Not Your Mothe...

On Dogs

Created by
Dahlynn McKowen,
Ken McKowen and Kathleene Baker

Published by
Publishing Syndicate

 PO Box 607
Orangevale California 95662
www.PublishingSyndicate.com

Not Your Mother's Book . . .
On Dogs

First Edition December 2012
Copyright 2012 by Publishing Syndicate LLC

*We would like to thank the many individuals
who granted us permission to reprint their stories.
See the complete listing beginning on page 262.*

Created and edited by Dahlynn McKowen,
Ken McKowen and Kathleene Baker
Cover and Book Design by Publishing Syndicate
Cover art: Stefanie Collins
Copyeditor: Terri Elders

Published by
Publishing Syndicate
PO Box 607
Orangevale California 95662

www.PublishingSyndicate.com
www.Facebook.com/PublishingSyndicate
Twitter: @PublishingSynd

Print Edition ISBN: 978-1-938778-06-3
Digital Edition ISBN: 978-1-938778-07-0
Library of Congress Control Number 2012921792

Printed in Canada

This book is a collaborative effort. Writers from all over the world submitted their work for consideration, with 57 stories making the final cut. All contributors are compensated for their stories and are invited to take part in a media campaign.

Publishing Syndicate strongly encourages you to submit your story to one of its many anthologies. You'll find information on how to do so at the end of this book, starting on page 272.

~~ To James M. Pearson ~~

Jim, as my husband Jerry and I called him, always had a smile on his face and a dog in his home. His first canine companion—El Pomar—opened many new doors for Jim, and provided many new life adventures, one being that his dog brought him and his future wife, Serena, together.

Jim left this world shortly after submitting his story for this book, a funny tale about one of his and El Pomar's many escapades. We invite you to laugh with us as you read the story for yourself, which begins on page 103.

And we would be remiss if we didn't thank Serena for helping us finalize Jim's story for publication. We are forever in your gratitude. Thank you.

~~ Kathleene Baker

Serena, Jim and El Pomar (Best Dog)

CONTENTS

3. Companions Like None Other   85

4. Unleashed   135

5. Dog Treats   183

Acknowledgments

Lots of people and doggies to thank, all around!

Our families:

Thank you to Kathleene's husband Jerry for both his unwavering support and never-ending patience as his wonderful wife plunged headfirst into the unknown world of authorship!

Thank you to Kathleene's father Raymond Boucher for sharing her excitement over the book and tolerating her making fewer trips to Kansas to visit him. Kathleene credits the wacky Boucher gene pool for helping her tackle this most recent challenge, and for that, she is grateful.

Thank you to Kathleene's fur kids Hank, Samantha and Abby. She promises you all more play time now that the book is done, and thanks you for lighting up her life each day.

And last, thank you to Dahlynn's teenage son Shawn for once again putting up with the general craziness another new book brings to the McKowen household.

And our extended family:

Thank you to Terri Elders for your superb copyediting work. You never fail to keep our company on track and moving right along!

Thank you to Pat Nelson for being Publishing Syndicate's proofreader extraordinaire. Are you having fun yet?

Thank you to Paul Krupin for overseeing our media and public relations campaign. Through your company Direct Contact PR (www.DirectContactPR.com), you have never let us down, helping us navigate the ever-evolving world of media and promotion.

Thank you to Lee Simonson, owner of online newsletters *Petwarmers* and *Heartwarmers*, for publishing Kathleene's first article, thus beginning an unforeseen but enjoyable journey.

Thank you to Patricia and Jim Frank of *FrankTalk*, Betty Keel of *Southern Tour* and Jennifer Deaves of GoodGabble. com for your continued support of Kathleene's writing.

Thank you to those many people—especially rescue and pet organizations—who generously hosted online story call-outs. Submissions swamped our database and left us with wagging tails! To all of you, a special "paws up!"

Thank you to our NYMB co-creators for joining us on this amazing journey. Your turn to create that book is coming soon, so get ready!

Most of all, thank you to those who graciously shared their stories with us. We wished we could have used all of them— but remember, there's still the sequel!

~~ Dahlynn McKowen, Ken McKowen and Kathleene Baker

Introduction

Outside of a dog, a book is man's best friend.
Inside of a dog, it's too dark to read.
~~ Groucho Marx

It never fails—the venerable Groucho Marx had a saying for everything. When I came across this one, I about laughed myself silly! It is a fitting quote for this very funny and entertaining book.

For many—especially us writers who live to put pen to paper about our dogs, and also for those of us who love to read about dogs—books and canines are a natural combo. To me, this combo is as American as apple pie and ice cream, cowboys and rodeos and back-to-back episodes of reality TV available on any given night. (My guilty pleasure is *Survivor*, which I watch with my three darling fur kids, while drinking wine and eating anything chocolate).

We are dog people. It's just as plain and as simple as that. While some may think we're a bit off our rockers—especially them cat people—we don't give a hoot. Our fur kids are our babies, our children. They are our trusted companions and know we will do them no harm. They ask for nothing in return. They shower us with their loyalty and are appreciative when we tend to their needs, from feeding time to play time. Our dogs are our sanity and help reduce our stress levels when it comes to our having to deal with everyday life—if they don't

drive us nuts with puppy-dog antics and silly canine adventures, many of which are shared in this title.

With that, it is now time to snuggle up with your favorite pooch and enjoy the stories within. And a tip of the old hat to Groucho—a dog *and* a book are two of man's best friends!

~~ Kathleene Baker

CHAPTER ONE

Puppy Love

From cute to chaotic!

A Boy and His Dog

by
Sioux Roslawski

The first time we saw her, she was being held up in the air—upside down—by a couple of boys. They gripped her around the belly as she squirmed to get loose. Feeling sorry for the little pup, we wondered what other roughness she'd endure if we didn't choose her.

Our family included a 10-year-old daughter named Virginia, a toddler son named Ian and a couple of cats. What we didn't have was a dog. My husband and I both believe that nothing teaches love and responsibility like having a dog.

Deciding on the breed was just as simple. Golden Retrievers are gentle, tolerant and have soft mouths . . . the kind of dog that doesn't bear down with their teeth and tear into skin. They're also gorgeous.

However, the price of a Golden Retriever was not compatible with our barely-making-it budget. No way did we have several hundred dollars to buy a puppy. After calling all the area Humane Society shelters and pounds looking for a Golden to rescue, we lowered our standards a bit. We decided to look for a Golden mix.

After poring over the papers, I found a possibility: a German Shepherd mama had supposedly hooked up with a Golden dad. Their offspring, offered for $20 each, were much more in our price range. My husband Michael's birthday was right around the corner. This would be a wonderful opportunity—a gift for him, and a dog for our entire family to love.

I made an appointment to see the litter after Virginia promised to keep our plan a secret. (Our son stayed with a baby sitter; he was so young that he surely would have blabbed.) When we arrived, unfortunately, the adults were not home. No problem, the kids assured us. When we said we wanted a pup that looked like a Golden and we preferred a female, they took us to their backyard. There was the mama dog watching as her puppies romped around. Some had the darker coloring of their mother, while a few of them were completely tan.

The child in charge chose one that took after the pup's daddy and hoisted it up into the air. They turned the puppy upside down to determine its gender. A female! They carried her over to the fence, where we stood watching.

Her coloring, for the most part, was what we wanted. She was completely tan, except for a thin stripe of black along her spine. She didn't appear as fluffy as we imagined Golden Retriever puppies to be, but we figured that the combination of a Shepherd's intelligence and a Golden's temperament would be a winner. We happily paid our $20 and whisked the puppy home. She was so tiny that she fit in my daughter's lap with room to spare.

Thrilled with his gift—even though it didn't have to be unwrapped and there was no surprise to it—Michael named her Trixie, after a character in his favorite television show, *The Honeymooners*. He asserted that if it had been a male, the name would have been Norton.

Although it was probably our imagination, it seemed as soon as we brought Trixie home, the black stripe down her back expanded. The fur never got thick and long but instead remained spindly and wiry, just like a German Shepherd's. And even though her body and head were clearly not pure Golden Retriever, her heart was pure gold.

Trixie lived to please us. She never did anything wrong. Oh, we still have a chair that bears teeth marks from her puppyhood, but other than that, she did nothing bad. Easy to potty train, she soon grew into a riding toy for our young son, Ian. She never jumped on the furniture, and we had to beg her to hop onto our bed. She'd oblige, reluctantly, but wouldn't stay long. It was as if she was saying to us, "You obviously want me up here, and I'll do it to make you happy, but I know, and you know, that a dog doesn't belong here." After snuggling with us for a while, she'd get down quietly and slink into the family room.

Trixie stopped growing after a year or so, while Ian shot up like a bean sprout. Even though Trixie was Michael's dog, Ian and Trixie had an unshakable bond. She was the first one Ian greeted when he got home from school in the afternoon. When he played ball in the backyard, Trixie tagged along to keep a protective eye on him. They were truly inseparable.

As Ian grew busier, the quantity of time he spent with Trixie changed, but qualitatively—not at all. When Ian walked into the house after soccer games or marching band practice, he always ruffled Trixie's fur or patted her on the head before vanishing into his bedroom for the evening. When our bottomless-pit-of-a-son prowled around in the kitchen foraging for food, if he saw Trixie mournfully standing over her empty water bowl, he'd ask, "Are you thirsty, girl?" and fill the water bowl to the brim. When it came to cheeseburgers or pizza, they were buddies as well; when Ian ate, so did Trixie—bits of pizza crust or a bite of a burger would invariably be tossed her way.

These days, my husband and I shake our heads when we see the two of them together. We feel like voyeurs, spying on a secret side of our son. Our boy, 6 feet of sinewy muscle, unbelievably aggressive on the soccer field or the tennis court—is invariably tender when he touches Trixie, who, in dog years, is now a senior citizen.

Careless and forgetful with his belongings—his book bag, his shoes, his trumpet mutes—Ian is the epitome of attentiveness when it comes to Trixie. Ian answers our questions with grunts and gestures and monosyllables. In his mind, a conversation with his parents measured in seconds, rather than minutes, is ideal. As for the tan, four-legged vacuum cleaner that usually can be found lying right in the middle of the hall? Ian has no problem lingering over her. He rubs her back, starts to walk away, and rethinking it, will return to give a few final pats.

Soon, we know, our boy will leave the nest. College is right around the corner. As we witness how excited Trixie gets every afternoon or evening when Ian comes home—her tail and rear end wagging with undiluted love—we wonder. How will Trixie react when she has to wait weeks, maybe even months, for Ian's homecomings? Will she know his absence is not due to his falling out of love with her, but instead is just a natural part of life? I have a feeling that every time they reunite, they will pick up right where they left off. She'll wag her entire butt in exuberance, he'll ruffle her fur, and all the years will disappear, revealing the only thing that's important in that moment—a boy and his dog.

Ian in first grade

Trixie over the ages

The Dutch Progeny

by
Kathe Campbell

We allowed ourselves less than 24 hours of bereavement. Some folks would view it impetuous and insensitive needing to replace a beloved friend so soon. But to a pair of dog lovers in our 70s, we dared not let too much time pass us by.

Losing any number of precious animals had been a part of living and dying on our ranch, but none had struck us harder. The older we were, the harder we fell. While holding our girl close at the veterinarian's, we two old fogies unabashedly allowed our tattered souls to choke back mournful tears, until we could hold them back no more.

Our beloved Keeshond had brought years of uncompromising joy as a herder and steady companion. At the shelter, her dark liquid eyes had pitifully begged, "Please, folks, take me home with you," and we had been smitten. None other would do, this Dutch barge dog, this silver-and-black treasure that asked nothing but to work, sit close and be loved unconditionally. She guarded us and our critters for 14 years and never left Ken's side when he fell seriously ill.

We left our veterinarian that morning with instructions to cremate and that we would be back later to pick up her remains. There was other essential business to tend to, which required a drive north. Throughout the five-hour trip, we struck up happy Keeshond chords, recalling our smart and devoted girl, in between helpless and woeful weeps. It was a dreadful scene.

Red-faced with hankies handy, we stopped at noon for a sandwich and a city newspaper. Finding too many downer headlines, I single-mindedly glanced at the want ads under "Pets." Finding the rare Keeshond was probably a silly notion, but in fierce loneliness and desperation, one grasps foolishly.

Then I saw it. Right there, before my eyes, was an ad posted by a veterinarian/dog breeder, who was located three hours south of our current location. The ad said there was one male Keeshond left in his current semiannual whelp. *Could it be?* I thought to myself. I called the number in the ad on my cell and asked if the pup was still available. He was! The person asked to come before 8 P.M., if possible. Someone up there had His eye on us two old crows. Excited waterworks overwhelmed us.

We continued on, completed our original business, with me all but dragging Ken in and out of his scheduled appointments, and made the long trip south to the vet's country kennel with a half-hour to spare. We searched the immaculate cages, but there were no Keeshonds in sight. Holding back disappointment, I felt a blast of heat rise from my pounding heart, washing red-hot over my face. "Someone must have taken the pup, Ken," I moaned to my husband, like a spoiled child.

"The Keeshonds are out for their evening stroll, ma'am," offered the doctor. "You must be the folks interested in our last Keesh pup."

I nearly kissed the poor man, while shoving half a dozen snapshots of our girl at him.

"Ah, yes, I too have a wonderful lady Keeshond over at the house, and in fact we've worn out three of them in our family," he said with a smile. "So I guess you already know their wonderful personalities, despite all the high maintenance in winter." We both nodded in complete understanding as the doctor headed out back to get the pup.

"Don't be so fidgety," whispered Ken while I paced and gazed impatiently at the outer door. Suddenly, the baby flew through the back door, his curly tail doing a jig atop his back. The doctor made the three of us comfortable in a private room for puppy slurps, excited baby whimpers and the love-light shining all around. I prayed that writing a check for a high-end figure wouldn't result in my dear Scotsman's burst of thrift, but Ken came through, for he agreed that this puppy was one beautiful little fellow.

While driving the 200 miles home listening to our favorite Western tunes on the XM satellite radio, together we sang, *A Boy Named Sue*. We also stopped a few times for father-and-son piddles in the darkness of nightfall.

"Sue," I mused out loud, trying to think of a name for our new baby as he slept soundly against my hip. Ken suggested "Corky" instead, after a great dog in our past. And so our new boy was christened "Corky Sue." I leaned back contentedly and somehow felt assured that our beloved lady had forgiven our haste in finding another Dutch descendant.

Corky Sue and Kathe

A Facebook Affair

by
Bobby Barbara Smith

It started very innocently on a December day in 2010. I was checking my favorite animal rescues on Facebook, expecting as usual to see numerous doggies in distress, some lost and many needing "forever" homes. I do what I can to spread the word, share the sweet faces and chip in financially when one pulls at my heartstrings.

On that particular day, I spotted an urgent post from Rocky Ridge Refuge, located in northern Arkansas. There in front of me were pictures of a litter of puppies and the mama dog, left outside in piles of trash during a frigid winter with no shelter or food.

Rocky Ridge was not set up for small dogs and these little Dorkies (Dachshund and Yorkie) were tiny compared to the Great Danes, Irish Wolfhounds and other large breeds at the refuge. The fenced areas there were to contain large dogs. The refuge knew once these little ones were up and running, they would need fosters, or better yet, forever homes.

I wasn't set up for fostering and I certainly wasn't looking for another dog. I had a grumpy, 11-year-old terrier who ruled the house with an iron paw and sharing wasn't in his DNA! But the plight of these little dogs stayed on my mind.

Janice Wolf, owner of Rocky Ridge Refuge, started the healing process, working her magic on each little Dorkie. Every morning, I jumped on Facebook, ignoring all other posts as I scurried to the RRR wall to read the latest Dorkie news. They were all adorable, but one little girl—the weakest one—had my attention. I'd search until I found her pictures and returned many times during the day to see her again. She wasn't the cutest of the bunch—her skin was in bad condition and she was very frail—but she had the sweetest face with eyes that spoke to my heart.

I wasn't the only one caught up in the Dorkie-web. Each day, I'd see inquiries, people wanting to adopt this one or that one. As the Dorkies healed, the posts went out for adoptions. I'd cheer along with others as the strongest began to find homes.

Janice worried over the long skinny girl, as did I. My morning was not complete until I found her sweet face staring out from under a Great Dane's ear or curled up in a puppy pile. Yes, I admit, this little girl was stealing my heart via Facebook.

One morning as I scanned the RRR news, I saw a post saying the little black female would be leaving that day for a forever home. Instead of cheering, my heart sank. I didn't know why, but I was overcome with sadness at the thought of never seeing her sweet face again.

Immediately I called Janice, my heart racing as I waited for her to answer. "Is she taking the little frail girl?" My voice was panic-stricken.

"No, and she's the sweetest one of all. I may keep her if no one shows interest," Janice replied. I began to breathe again.

Then I heard words gushing from my mouth. "Oh, I so love her, but my husband would not hear of it! My Cairn would pack his bones and leave home, but I can't get her out of my brain!"

Now, Janice was a clever one. She knew what was destined to be long before I had a clue.

"Well, you could help me out by fostering her over Christmas. That would give me a break and she'd be out of the danger of these large paws stepping on her. Tell your husband it's temporary, you're just fostering her for the holidays, and then let the little doll work her magic on him. If she needs to come back to RRR, she can."

My heart jumped with excitement. My husband might just go for that, even though when I'd shown him her sweet pictures, he always replied, "We don't need another dog!" However, this way I'd be helping Janice and giving this sad little dog a good Christmas, which she most certainly deserved. How could he deny her that?

The plan was hatched and set into motion. My husband agreed and gave me a long I-know-what-you're-up-to look, but I didn't care. I would pick up Maggie May (yes, I named her), but first I had shopping to do and a house to puppy-proof.

Finally the day arrived and I drove to Rocky Ridge with assorted pink toys, a pink collar, leash, blanket and treats. I wanted this little girl to like me. "Oh, what if she doesn't like me," I agonized aloud, driving through the gate and up the hill to the refuge.

My worries were soon put to rest. Janice carried a precious bundle out to me and I knew from the moment she placed her in my arms, I'd never let her go.

And so, Miss Maggie May came bouncing into our world for the holiday break, with silky ears flopping and her sweet pink tongue kissing, kissing and kissing. Oh my goodness!

You never know what kind of baggage a rescue dog will own, but Maggie May was a gem. She picked up walking on-leash instantly and had only one accident in the house. On her second day when she went zooming into the room where my rescued blue jays lived—don't ask, that's a whole different story—Maggie May must have looked like a cat to them and they thought they were under siege. Typical of jays, they screamed their "cat attack" warning calls, one after another. Poor Maggie froze and lost all bodily functions. She then dropped to her belly in fear. I raced to help her and my heart broke.

"Oh, baby, nothing will ever hurt you!" I scooped her up and assured her that it was not her fault. I truly understood. Sometimes when I'm in close proximity to the jays' fly cages and they let out that squawk . . . well, let's just say it's enough to shake the strongest bladder!

During her stay with us, Maggie May began the process of wrapping my hubby around her perfect little paws. It didn't take long—he tried to ignore her, but caved almost immediately. Soon our little girl was getting back rubs and ear scratches from the old softy.

Indy, my grumpy old terrier, took much longer to warm up to Maggie May. He wasn't aggressive toward her, he'd just move away with a disgusted look when she tried to play, and he refused to look at her. I think he reasoned, "If I don't see her, she will go away!" When she didn't, he would glare at me from across the room, especially when I spoke to her or paid her any attention in his presence.

I felt confident that Maggie's sweetness would eventually take care of the situation. It didn't happen overnight, but I could see him weakening in his stubborn standoff. She would curl up in his huge bed, all comfy, while he suffered on the hard floor. It was a great day when I looked to see them both sleeping on the same bed. If you've ever owned a stubborn dog, you know what a big deal this was!

One morning over coffee, my husband and I were watching Maggie systematically dragging all of her toys out of the toy basket, and marveling at how happy she seemed.

"You know she's not going back to Rocky Ridge, don't you?" I queried.

"I knew that before she got here," my hubby said, chuckling smugly.

OK, so I wasn't as clever as I thought I was, but this I know—Maggie and I were destined to be together.

Maggie May still has a few fears locked in her little mind from the days when she and her littermates were left to their own defenses. Only they know for sure the horrors they endured, and I never know what might trigger that fear. However, she is healing and doesn't frighten nearly as frequently as in the beginning.

I learned something very valuable about healing and rescues. It's almost always a two-way process. I thought I was saving Maggie, but along the way I realized she was saving me. I had lost a son to cancer in 2009 and thought I was doing OK under the circumstances. I didn't really know how badly I needed this little girl to care for, to curl up with in a chair, and to love. When I get too sad, she will pounce on me from out of nowhere, dissolving my tears into bursts of laughter! You cannot stay sad for long with such a joyful girl peeking out from under the covers, leaping over toy baskets and kissing... always the kissing!

I saw a picture of a rescue dog the other day with the caption, "I rescued a human today." And that's exactly what Maggie May did for me—all due to a posting on my Facebook page.

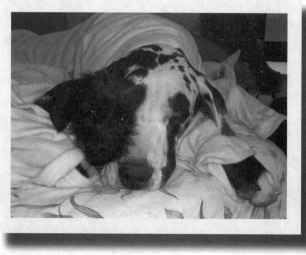

Maggie May and her great big friend

Dream Girl

by
Elynne Chaplik-Aleskow

My sisters and I stood at the living room window and watched my father get out of the car. He was holding a brown cardboard box. In anticipation, my 2-year-old sister, Susan, took one look at the box and promptly threw up. She was terrified of all dogs.

My dad entered the apartment holding the box. He lowered it so I could see what was inside, and that was the first moment I saw our new German Shepherd—"Dream Girl."

It was a hot summer afternoon and my cousins Eddie and Larry were visiting our family. Being the tomboy that I was, seeing them was always a special treat. However, my other sister Linda always complained that during our games of Cowboys and Indians, she was the first to get killed off.

I picked up the new puppy and we headed to our backyard to play Rin Tin Tin. We were utterly amazed at how quickly Dream Girl became one of us. Every time we shot Linda and she fell to the ground, our genius puppy would go to her and put a paw on her body.

We were playing for an hour or so when Dream Girl collapsed. We all ran and stood over her in a circle. She did not move. I ran into the apartment yelling for my father to come.

"The puppy is dead!" I screamed.

He hurried to the yard and informed us that playing in the hot sun had caused the puppy to faint. He explained that she needed shade and water. "Remember," he cautioned, "she is just a baby."

Although Linda and I were very comfortable with this quickly growing puppy, Susan kept her distance and was increasingly afraid. We had a knotty-pine den in the apartment with a full door that could be used as a half door—one could close the bottom half and leave the upper half open. Very early one morning, while my parents and I were asleep, Linda was in the den playing with Dream Girl. Susan watched from what she considered the safe side of the half-opened door.

Stroking Dream Girl, Linda taunted Susan. "I dare you to come in here and pet this dog. I know you're a scared baby and will never come close to the dog."

"I am not a baby," Susan cried.

"Then prove it," Linda, the young psychologist, countered.

Sure enough, when my parents and I awoke, there was Susan proudly petting the gentle Shepherd. Linda stood next to them both with a smile of triumph. It was the end of Susan's fear of dogs.

Dream Girl was to become my closest friend and I loved her with all my heart.

My family moved to a house the next year. Unfortunately,

my mother was not a dog lover. With our new white carpet, Dream Girl was only allowed in certain rooms of the house.

One afternoon, while my mother was out shopping, Dream Girl and I had the run of the house. Unfortunately, I did not hear my mom's car pull into the driveway in time to bring Dream Girl downstairs. When Mom came inside, she found Dream Girl and me playing in her white-carpeted living room. She started yelling at me to get the dog out of there. Dream Girl, startled and frightened, began urinating on my mother's new carpeting. The more my mother yelled, the more my dog urinated while running in circles around the room as I tried to catch her. Both Dream Girl and I were in the doghouse over that episode.

One night there was a terrible rainstorm. The lightening was blinding and the thunder was deafening. As I walked downstairs to the garage, I saw water seeping in under the door. My first thought was of Dream Girl—she was out in the garage. As I opened the door, my mother yelled, "Don't open that door!"

Nothing could have kept me from my dog. The water in the flooded garage knocked me over as it swiftly entered the house. Swimming on top of it was my precious dog. She swam to me and started licking me as I sat soaked on the floor. I held her tight and kissed her back.

My mother was so distracted by the flood she didn't even notice Dream Girl and me head upstairs to my bedroom. I took a towel and tenderly dried her. That night she slept with me in my room.

My dad had a German Shepherd when he was a boy. He loved them. His dog appeared on his doorstep one night during a storm, so he called him "Stormy." This dog became my father's personal protector. One day, a buddy of Dad's came up behind him and playfully put a chokehold on him. Stormy plunged toward the boy and if my dad had not caught the leash, the dog would have attacked. Dad was always convinced that Stormy was a lost military dog. Then one day, as he came, so he left.

When my father bought Dream Girl, her papers stated she was the great, great granddaughter of Rin Tin Tin III. I was very proud of this pedigree. Even so, my dad claimed she was not as smart as his dog because he had trouble housebreaking her. I, on the other hand, thought she was not only smart but as loving and attentive as one could hope for in any sensitive friend. Her name fit her well. And although she belonged to the family, there was no doubt in my mind she was my dog.

As life would have it, I dearly love dogs, but Dream Girl has been my only dog. As an adult, I have lived in a condo building that does not allow animals, but has the most beautiful views of Chicago. It is a hard choice to have made to stay here because I desperately want a dog—but the view is priceless.

I live along the lake where there is a dog beach I visit often. I am the only one there without a dog. Whenever I see a German Shepherd, I stop and lovingly stroke the memory of my Dream Girl.

The Right Doorstep

by
Joanne Gardner

I stepped back a few paces while wiping my hands, black with potting soil, on the rear of my jeans. "Perfect!"

The oversized doorstep that I'd always envisioned, large enough for numerous potted plants, seemed to shout, "Welcome, it's springtime in Texas!" The new entrance had been my husband's latest project and I was anxious for him to see the display I had created. It was eye-popping!

The phone rang and I scooted inside the house.

"Hi, honey!" My husband's voice sounded unusual.

"Hi, Jack. What's going on?"

"Umm, I need to tell you something, Joanne. Well, I need to ask you something," he stammered. "Oh, never mind, I'm just a few miles away. It's a long story."

There was angst in the tone of his voice, the very tone he uses when expecting us to disagree. I braced myself. *What now?* I thought to myself. *Was he dragging home another flea market treasure? Another old vehicle to rebuild? What? WHAT THIS TIME?*

Shortly I heard his truck pulling into the driveway. I opened the door to see Jack and a young pup standing on our newly constructed doorstep, now abundant with various sized pots of colorful plantings. The pooch shimmied from head to toe while peering up at me—while Jack, with his head hung low, stood motionless, looking just like a sad whipped pup.

"Jack, what are you thinking? Where did this baby come from?"

There was a long pause. "Don't say no yet! She seems perfectly healthy so we aren't looking at major medical expenses and she needs a home."

I sighed and replied gently but firmly, "No. Absolutely not. We won't be keeping this one. I'm sorry but there has to be a limit. We will, however, take care of her temporarily— she'll not be going to a shelter."

She truly was the cutest and most innocent-looking baby ever. I knelt to her level, stroked her silky ears, gazed into soft, beautiful eyes and she gave kisses with wild abandon. I swear her eyes peered right into my soul. Her breed was that of Catahoula, and she may as well have spoken English for I swear I heard her ask, "Can I live here and will you love me forever?" I felt like a heathen and I hadn't done one thing wrong. Dogs do that to me.

I noticed she had a collar but no tags so I was sure she wasn't a stray—she was someone's lost pet. After working in a veterinary clinic for many years, I knew Catahoula pups were not typically strays.

"We need to make posters and call local vets. This pup is simply lost, Jack."

He spoke around the lump in his throat, "Joanne, I saw the jerk dump her out of his truck and speed off."

The three of us sat in the grass under a shade tree to discuss the dreadful situation. The pup rolled onto her back for a tummy rub, and then clamored over us time and time again, tripping and falling with big, clumsy feet she hadn't yet grown into. Could she possibly make herself anymore precious? *Darn her*, I thought.

Jack told me the story, for he had witnessed the whole event. The pup's owner had opened the passenger door, pushed her out and sped away. The dog stood and watched until the truck was out of sight. Frightened, she began to pace, cry and spin in circles, not knowing which way to go. Jack, only a short distance away, whistled, called, clapped his hands and knelt down as if wanting to play. At the sound of a human, her ears perked up and she dashed down the road so quickly her legs were a blur, as was her wagging tail. She crashed into Jack so hard he fell backwards and the joyful pup's slobbery kisses began.

Little did she know that Jack was a man whose heart melts at the sight of any and all needy critters. Jack lifted her into his truck and headed for home. She snuggled close, and then inch by inch, she slowly slid down onto the seat while drifting into la-la land, her head resting upon Jack's leg.

Hearing the pup's pitiful story, my heart sank and my ire rose. How could anyone be so damned cruel! However, I had to put my foot down. We have found, rescued or been given almost every breed known to mankind, including several Heinz

57 varieties. It seems the only requirement to find a home with us is to possess four legs and sport a fur coat. With retirement nearing and already spending a near fortune on pets, even with my employee discount, we didn't need another. A good home for a Catahoula pup would not be difficult to find, especially with my work at the vet clinic.

"OK, we'll talk over dinner. Time to go inside. This baby probably needs food and water and I need to start cooking."

When we opened the front door, Ava Gardner, our reigning queen from hell who we cleverly had lent our last name to, came screeching and yapping down the hallway. With wild, silky hair trailing behind her, upper lip curled and teeth bared, she was coming in for the kill. Excited to see another dog, the pup let go with a deep *woof.* Ava slammed on her brakes and skidded to a halt. The quizzical look on her face was as stupid as her behavior. Maybe it was her name—that of a celebrity— that made her such a snit. Would her personality have developed differently had she been called Maude or Bertha?

Ava had joined our family as a tiny Yorkshire Terrier puppy several years prior. At the time we had two gigantic, older Russian Wolfhounds. Both soon learned Ava *thought* she ruled the roost and they allowed her to fantasize she was the leader of the pack. They couldn't have cared less when she scolded, snarled, snapped or yanked toys from their mouths . . . they let her get away with murder. Thus, we lived with a tiny dog from hell, loved her to pieces and were thankful she allowed us to remain on our own premises.

Before we'd even had dinner, Ava and the pup made a peace treaty of sorts. And before we crawled into bed that night, I'd eaten a gigantic piece of humble pie. I first weakened and said that *maybe* the pup could stay, only to change my mind within a matter of minutes. No way would that fur baby go anywhere. Just before falling asleep, I sat straight up in bed. "Her name will be 'Nan!'" I announced to my husband.

"'Nan?' Where'd that come from? What a stupid name, Joanne!"

"Remember when you asked if we could keep her? Do you remember what I said?"

"Certainly, and I didn't like it. You said, 'No, absolutely not!' How could I forget?" Jack snarled.

He must have picked that up from Ava, I thought, smiling inside. I explained to Jack how I had come up with her name, taking the first letter from each word in "No, absolutely not." I giggled at my own wit before rolling over to go to sleep.

Just as I was dozing off I heard Jack murmur, "Maybe we could just call her 'Maybe?'"

I ignored his smart remark and fell asleep.

With Nan's arrival, prissy Ava took to her bed for three days. Our king-sized bed, that is! She guarded it fiercely, racing full speed up one side, down the other and across the foot if sweet Nan even neared the bed. On the fourth day, Nan bravely laid her head on the foot of the bed and Ava went berserk. "This is my bed. You're just a newcomer!" she snarled, grumbled and charged. Within days Nan was on to her and didn't bat an eyelash at her wacky ways, although Ava continued her foolish conduct in hopes someone might notice.

Nan did come with a few issues, but only typical puppy behavior. Within the first few weeks, she ate two pairs of Jack's expensive leather loafers and three pairs of my house slippers. Luckily, I worked for a vet clinic. You know—in case Nan found herself with serious issues related to her eating disorder.

Trying to satisfy Nan's chewing habits, we bought expensive toys like they were going to be discontinued—the type guaranteed not to break regardless of breed. Yep, she destroyed all of them. We ran ourselves ragged returning parts of the toys for promised refunds. Local pet store clerks came to know us on a first-name basis. How nice. And I learned to never misplace a receipt.

With pups come baby gates. Nan required nearly as many baby gates as we had rooms. Our home looked like an obstacle course for the first year of her life. Yet, when she wasn't causing havoc, she was a true lover. From day one she decided to be a lap dog like Ava. By the time Nan hit 70 pounds, she had a difficult time with laps and often slid off right onto the floor. But accepting defeat was NOT in her gene pool. She squirmed, tightened up into a ball, and usually managed to remain in place until the circulation in our legs came to a dead halt.

When we thought the worst of Nan's puppyhood was over, I discovered a disorder I came to call *kitchen kleptomania* and it kept me in a quandary. Closing off the dog door might have solved the problem, but did I really want to trade out for a possible potty accident? I considered signing Nan up for obedience school, hoping they would have some sort of specialized therapy for her condition. I swore if I continued to find forks, knives and spoons in the backyard, I'd just sign up for therapy myself, especially since I never once caught Nan snatching utensils from the table or dishwasher. Luckily she didn't gnaw on them—she simply decorated the backyard with pretties that sparkled in the sunshine. It was like Christmas every day, with Nan in charge of outside décor, her color scheme being green and silver.

Some people pick up poop before mowing. We pick up poop, knives, forks and spoons. That is, Jack picks up the poop—while I retrieve our eating utensils. Yes, life is good at the Gardner's, each day is much like visiting the funny farm.

Nan was fortunate to join the ranks of a very happy pack that includes an 11-year-old mixed breed named "Mutley," two gentle cats named "Tucker" and "Bye Bye," and two adults who are suckers for all critters. And, of course, there's the ever-reigning queen from hell—Ava Gardner. By the way, Ava finally relented and Nan is now allowed on the bed. Big of her, huh?

When that sweet bundle of joy was thrown out like yesterday's newspaper, she definitely landed on the right doorstep!

Daughter Knows Best

by
Kathy Whirity

Our daughter Jaime and her husband, Dan, stopped over for an unannounced visit one evening. In Jaime's arms was a new addition to their family—a sweet black-and-white Border Collie that fit perfectly in the palm of my hand. She had been named "Maizy," an unusual, catchy name that fit her like no other could. There was only one problem—Hannah. Our 5-year-old Golden Retriever wanted nothing to do with the likes of a new puppy.

Soon Jaime began hounding us to get another dog. There was a method to her manipulation. She wanted a playmate for Maizy. We tried to remain steadfast in our decision to remain a one-dog family.

Jaime searched and searched until she found a breeder with excellent credentials. She hoped to change my mind by sharing the information she had gathered. The facts were that the Golden Retriever parents were service dogs, loving and gentle, and for this male and female, it was their first litter.

"Mom, how can you pass this up?" Jaime asked. She was more than hopeful she could change my mind. And she now had an ally in her goal to bring home a 6-week-old pup for her dad on Father's Day—her younger sister, Katie, would also chip in for the present of a fluffy new puppy. It didn't take long for my husband Bill and me to ponder the possibility that maybe this canine connection was divine providence. Maybe it was meant to be after all.

Father's Day dawned and we were ready to meet our newest fur kid. I gasped with excitement to see a tiny ball of reddish-brown fluff come bounding down the gangway and right into my open arms. It was love at first sight and he was named "Henry." Just as Jaime had hoped, Maizy and Henry bonded immediately and become best buddies.

We spent hours simply watching the canine clowns at play. They alternated tug of war with rubber bones, to games of chase from one end of the house to the other. When they eventually tired of the frolicking, they laid side-by-side, content to chew on the same rawhide bone, each claiming an end.

Today, when Henry comes charging full speed into my lap, I simply cannot imagine life without him. He is a big lug of a dog who has even managed to win over Hannah, although she still likes to prove she's the princess pooch of our home.

Maizy is a frequent visitor. When Jaime calls to say they're coming over, that's my cue to put on a pot of coffee and to make sure doggie toys are spread out for the canine cousins. Then it's time to sit back and spend some quality time with my family and fur-kin alike.

Henry, Hannah and Maizy are a flurry of four-legged mischief and fun whenever they're together. I'm thankful that I relented to my daughter's persistence we needed another dog. And Henry is much more than a playmate for Maizy—he is truly the dog of my dreams, my perfect pet.

Hmm . . . maybe my daughter did know best after all.

The Dump

By
Pat Nelson

Last year, my friend Nona and I visited a small town in Mexico. One reason for the trip was because I wanted to enjoy a sunny vacation before adding a puppy to the family. My husband Bob and I had started checking the ads for the perfect dog prior to my leaving. It had been nearly 45 years since I had owned a dog, so I knew I'd have to stay around home awhile for some training . . . for my own training as much as the pup's.

Nona and I walked to dinner along cobblestone streets in San Blas, Mexico and she stopped to pet every sad-eyed dog she saw. As we neared the restaurant, Nona heard music and wanted to dance. "Let's go there after dinner," she suggested.

I glanced across the street while we enjoyed our meal and read the name of the place she wanted to go dancing: *El Basurero*. "Hmm," I said. "Sounds like the word for 'dump.' That place is called 'The Dump!'" We both laughed.

After dinner, we wandered into El Basurero. The music

was loud, but not live. Collections of empty beer bottles stood on each white plastic table.

We sat down and ordered a beer, even though I don't care for the taste of the stuff. Nona bebopped in her plastic chair, enjoying the music. Soon, one of the patrons came over and asked her to dance. She accepted. My friend had some moves I had never seen before. She danced and danced, and when the song finally ended, the 10 or so customers in the bar cheered and applauded.

Between songs, we talked some more about my future pet. "I like big dogs," I said. "Something like a Great Dane, but smaller."

The waitress was a cute young gal in hot-pink shorts. She did her best to communicate with us. She told us her name was "Brisa" (pronounced "Brē sah"), which I found out later meant *breeze* in Spanish. Nona continued to dance, either with one of the patrons or with the waitress. It was obvious that the small crowd was amazed to see a lady over 60 dancing like a 20-year-old.

I don't dance, but with the encouragement of a second beer and Brisa, I finally lost my inhibitions and decided to try. As if on cue, an old whiskered guy with bare feet wandered over and offered me his weathered hand. I accepted. I kicked off my shoes and danced with him on the dirty, beer-stained floor of The Dump.

On the way home, we stopped at the town square and bought ice cream, even though it didn't mix too well with beer. As we strolled through the square enjoying our treat, an unkempt brown dog, with a hungry look in his eyes, came up to Nona. Soon we had both handed over our ice cream to the canine.

After my trip, Bob and I remained on the lookout for the perfect female dog, but we hadn't yet chosen a name for her. We live in a Spanish-style house on a horseshoe-shaped lake, and a large stone slab in our front yard has the name *Casa Herradura* (horseshoe house) carved into it. Our cat, too, has a Spanish name. He is named "Peso" because our aunt bought him at a garage sale for not much more than a peso. It seemed that our future puppy should have a Spanish name also. One day, when we talked about who would clean up after our soon-to-be new dog when she took a dump, I thought of my visit to The Dump in Mexico and the friendly waitress named Brisa. "That's it," I said. "We'll call her 'Brisa.'"

Finally, I saw an ad on Craigslist for a Great Dane and Labradoodle mix. There were 17 pups in the litter. Both males and females were available, some with smooth hair and some with curly coats. All except one were black with a tiny bit of white, and one was brown. "You'll fall in love with them," said Sandy, their owner. "When would you like to see them?"

A few days later, we made the long drive to Newberg, Oregon, to see the pups. The mama dog had been taken to the neighbor's house so we wouldn't make her nervous. The pups' daddy, a golden Labradoodle named George, met us at the door with a sideways grin and a wagging tail.

Sandy directed us to the living room where we could see the pups. The homeowners had pushed the furnishings to the edge of the room and they had put up a low fence to turn the remainder of the room into a kennel. Some pups slept in a pile while others nudged each other playfully. We wanted a small female, so Sandy picked up one curly little girl and handed her to Bob. She quickly quieted in his arms.

One puppy stood alone and she was the one that really stood out to me. She had a smooth, glossy coat. I'd never seen such a shiny coat. "Is that a female?" I asked.

"Yes," replied Sandy, "and she is one of the smaller ones. We call her 'Scarlett.' See the red ribbon around her neck?"

She put the pup in my arms.

"Come back here, Carrot," Sandy said to the pup with the orange ribbon. "Lime Green, where are you going?" The one my husband held was Pink Puppy. Only one did not require an identifying ribbon. That was Brown Puppy, the only one in the litter that was not black and white.

After holding both Scarlett and Pink Puppy, I just had to have Scarlett. We paid a deposit and arranged to pick her up on Memorial Day weekend. "But her name will be Brisa, not Scarlett," I said.

Brisa quickly became a spoiled girl. Bob cut a piece of heavy felt into a collar of large flower petals and when Brisa wore it, he called her his daisy dog. She loved the daisy collar, but I told her she should feel embarrassed to wear it around other dogs.

I didn't want Brisa to be a house dog, so we converted a storage room at one end of the house into her doghouse. It was heated and made a cozy bedroom for her. She often sat in a patio chair and sometimes even stood on the patio table to look out over the lake. But eventually she outgrew the patio chair. A search on Craigslist turned up one of those big old Papasan chairs, which made a perfect lounge chair for her.

I still wasn't willing to let her sleep inside, but when she injured her foot, that changed everything. I put her bed on the floor in our bedroom, but let her lie on our bed with us for a little while each evening before we went to sleep. When I was ready for her to move to her own bed, I told her to go to bed, and surprisingly she hopped off ours and went to her own. She has been doing that every night since, and yes, she is now a house dog.

None of my friends would have guessed that I'd allow a dog whose name I got at The Dump to sleep in my bed!

Pat, Bob and Brisa

Shiver Me Timbers

by
Carol Brosowske

The year was 1974. Jim and I were newlyweds, just start-ing our lives together. He was from a family that didn't care for pets, and I'd grown up in a home that was never without a dog. Those first six weeks of marriage were blissfully happy, but to me there was just a little something missing. There was no doubt what it was either—it was a dog. I didn't consider a house a home without a dog or two.

I spotted an ad in the local newspaper for Miniature Schnauzer puppies. It was a good-sized litter, five puppies, just over six-weeks-old. Did I dare? Yes, I dared! I told Jim I was going shopping and hightailed it out of the house before he could offer to go along. It wasn't really a lie—but it was going to be one heck of a surprise.

When I arrived at the proper address, I found there were five little babes to choose from. I cuddled the first one that approached me. He licked my face and when I looked into his eyes—my heart skipped a beat or two. I fell head over heels within minutes.

On my drive home I was a nervous wreck, Jim was not going to be happy. I was in for trouble—I knew it without a doubt. I worried that our first knock-down-drag-out as a married couple was going to be over the precious bundle sleeping in my lap. Once home, I took a deep breath and cautiously walked into the house, my heart pounding. The moment I pulled that tiny, furry, bundle of joy from beneath my sweater, Jim turned to mush. I was stunned when he all but yanked that baby from my arms and I'd never felt such relief. Whew, I'd pulled it off and we had a puppy.

We named our new fur kid "Barney." Not yet financially able to begin a family, he was the best thing to come into our lives. We couldn't keep our hands off him. And Jim soon wondered how he had survived a childhood that didn't include a dog.

Before that homecoming day was over, Jim was singing to our new pup. He made up a cute little ditty that included Barney's name and sang it numerous times a day. Once Barney knew his name, he knew it was his song. He'd scamper about, letting go with tiny, shrill, excited *yips*. It wasn't long before he added running in circles while being serenaded, still joining in with his off-key *yips*. He and Jim loved their jam sessions but I considered buying earplugs. Holy crap...I loved them both dearly but nearly went berserk when they broke into song. Jim never could carry a tune in a bucket, and he was crooning constantly.

To top things off, Barney had issues when it came to barking—he didn't sound like any dog I'd ever heard. However, he had several versions of expressing himself, and he did so loudly. Very loudly. He yapped, yipped, or yodeled at the doorbell, trash truck and other dogs walking past our home. Sometimes, I'm positive he simply liked to hear himself, sure that his canine voice sounded tough. How wrong he was. He sounded rather wimpy—and how many dogs yodel anyway? Besides which, he didn't bark at the times he should have. As in when needing to go outside—or alerting us that he wanted to come back inside. Possibly he was a few Milk Bones short of a full box when it came to communication skills.

We lived in Chicago where winters were cruel and harsh. Going outside to take care of business was grueling for a tiny, bitty boy being house-trained. You betcha, Barney learned to do both jobs quickly! Still, he came to the door shivering, shaking and often looked like a quivering icicle. We'd bring the frozen baby inside immediately and rub him down with a towel until he was warm and dry again. He loved the attention and doggie-massage. As a matter of fact, he shivered at the door both summer and winter but I gave it little thought—probably because Chicago summers seemed very mild to me after growing up in west Texas. Therefore, we catered to Barney's whims year 'round like the fools we were. He had us under his thumb . . . er, paw!

When Barney was 3 years old, we moved back to Texas with stifling summers but mild winters. Once we were into the dog-days of the summer, we noticed that even though it was 105 degrees outside, Barney was still at the door shivering as if he were freezing to death. What the heck was going on? Could he possibly be acting? Our dog, acting? Never heard of such a thing! Surely it wasn't so, but we put him to the test.

I let him outside one wicked day when the sun was blinding. There wasn't a hint of breeze—not one leaf moved and the thermometer read 107. When Barney spotted us glancing out the window, he'd come to the door and go into full-blown shivering/shaking mode. Yet if we hid from his view, he stood at the door like a normal canine—in fact, we saw him panting! Yep, he was putting on a show for us and had been for years. We'd been outsmarted by a spoiled rotten Miniature Schnauzer.

Truthfully, it was our fault that Barney didn't learn to bark at the door—we didn't give him the chance nor did we encourage him. What kind of pet parents were we anyway? Poor fella, how often did he sit at the door in agony, waiting until we noticed he had his back legs crossed? Not an easy task for a dog. If he could have, I'm sure he'd have grumbled, "Open the damned bathroom door for Pete's sake."

Yep, Barney was an actor—he starred in his very own production of *Shiver Me Timbers*, each and every day of his life. Do they give Academy Awards to dogs? If so, I'm positive he'd have won the coveted statue.

Carol and Barney

Dog People

by
Maggie Lamond Simone

Isn't it funny how some people seem obsessed with their pets? They treat them like they're human or something. In fact, *USA Today* published the results of a survey of 1,100 pet owners which suggested that things might just be getting a little bit out of control.

Let me begin by admitting that yes, I am a dog owner—a normal, average person who happens to love dogs. It does not make me obsessed, and when I refer to him—Decker—as my first-born, it does not mean that I harbor the illusion of having actually given birth to him. I mean, really. Everyone knows I was just the breathing coach.

However, we do have the same hair color, all right? Of course we do. He's a Golden Retriever. I'm a redhead. I didn't plan it. In fact, I've often read that people grow to look like their pets over time. Look it up. Any resemblance to L'Oreal Copper is pure coincidence.

And yes, I can be a little defensive about him. For instance, my mother was visiting when Decker and I first moved into my husband's house, and she commented on his lovely furnishings and carpeting.

"He obviously takes very good care of his things," she said, "and dog hair all over the place could upset him. You might have to think about getting rid of him at some point," she continued gently.

"Mom!" I said, shocked and horrified. "I can't get rid of him! It's his house, for Pete's sake!"

She looked at me in wonderment. "I meant the dog, honey."

None of this, however, indicates that I have an unusual or unnatural affection for my pet, any more so than a golfer could be accused of obsessing simply because he once wrapped his club around a tree. (See, honey? I told you. Everything's OK.)

I think it's completely possible to be passionate about something and yet remain within the realm of the reasonable, which is exactly why this survey was so amusing. I think you'd have to agree with me that there's something very wrong with these pet owners. You almost have to feel sorry for them.

The survey said, for instance, that 87 percent of pet owners include their pet in holiday celebrations and almost 100 percent buy them holiday gifts. That's just ridiculous. Does that mean the other 13 percent don't think that buying them gifts counts as including them in the celebration? Pshaw.

Then there are those who consider themselves their pet's mommy or daddy. That's just silly. Yes, it's easier than saying, "Come on, baby—come to the woman who feeds you, bathes you, walks you and takes you to the vet every other week!" But it's still silly.

And those who think their pet is "smart" or a "genius"? Get real. It's a pet, OK? And besides, can your dog spell? Mine can. Now that's a smart dog.

Of course, the 53 percent who take time off work to care for a sick pet are just being realistic. It's either that or you take time off work to clean up the carpet and floor because you didn't take time off to care for your sick pet. Please, people. Use your heads here. It's all common sense.

And the 52 percent who prepare special meals for their pet or celebrate their pet's birthday? Common sense again. Would you give dog food to your child? Of course not. Would you ignore your child's birthday? Again, of course not. If you care about someone (er, something), that kind of thoughtlessness simply does not happen.

As for the 43 percent who display their pet's photo at work, all I can say is, what's the matter with you? That means that 57 percent have no photos of their pets at work! What's the problem? No bulletin board? Office policy? Ashamed? I don't mind saying I have several pictures of Decker on my desk, right in front of—er, next to!—the picture of my family.

CHAPTER TWO

Every Dog Has Its Day

We all have our ups and downs.

The Beagle that Came in From the Rain

by
Gregory Lamping

My brother, who lives in the country, called to tell me about a Beagle that had been hanging around his cabin the past few weeks. He wanted to know if I would be interested in giving him a home. I told him, "No way." The last dog I would ever want to adopt was another Beagle. My first dog was a Beagle that would follow a scent to the ends of the earth and growl at anyone who disturbed his nap.

"Keep in mind," he said, before hanging up, "around here they shoot strays."

He knew that would prod me into taking action. I looked up Beagle Rescue and other groups that might help this dog find a home. I compiled a list and called my brother back, telling him that I'd take the dog and see what I could do.

On a rainy January evening, I drove out to my brother's cabin. The moment I saw the dog, my heart sank. *No one's going to want him*, I thought. *He's too ugly.* His neck was too long, his legs too short, his ribs were showing and the area under his nose was pink and raw.

Once I brought him home, he ran into the house and immediately began spraying on the furniture. I screamed and rushed for the paper towels. While wiping up the mess, I heard a commotion in the kitchen. He had knocked over the wastebasket searching for food. I quickly picked him up and carried him to the backyard.

After cleaning up the trash he had scattered about, I went outside to check on him. I looked around the yard and spotted him going down the sidewalk across the street with his nose to the pavement. He had slipped under the gate.

By the time I opened the front door, he had moved on. I got in my car and drove around the neighborhood searching for him, but with the hope that someone else would come upon this dog and find him a home, even if it were a dog shelter. I wanted to wipe my hands of him.

Then I saw him, sniffing around in a yard several blocks away. I pulled over and got out of the car. In the cold, drizzling rain, I yelled out, "Hey, you!" since I had yet to come up with a name for him. He stopped and looked back. Once he saw who I was, he raced over to me without hesitating for a second, wagging his tail.

I took him back home and put him on the deck. He was going to have to spend the night outside, since I didn't want to risk him spraying on more furniture or knocking over any more wastebaskets.

During the night, I got up to see how he was doing.

Behind the glass door, I saw him sitting there looking up at me. He was wet from the rain, but that didn't dampen the excitement in his eyes upon seeing me. I opened the door, let him in, and went back to sleep.

In the morning, I rolled over in bed and felt something. I opened my eyes and saw him sleeping like a baby next to my pillow. Looking at him, I realized that I had been blind—I had never seen a dog so beautiful. Right then and there, I knew he was mine. I named him "Scooter."

My new friend had finally found the one thing all dogs need more than anything else.

He had found a home.

Gregory and Scooter

A Higher Power than the Law

by

Sioux Roslawski

Wearing latex gloves and my son's huge hoodie, I knew that if I got caught, my face would be plastered all over the evening news and I would probably be fired from my job. Sadly, I am notoriously *not* photogenic—in the harsh lights at a police station, I could not even imagine the horrifying results.

I was there—stealing—for my friend, Susan. She and I had been writing colleagues for years. We passed each other stories to critique, and we bounced ideas off one another. She had even volunteered at my creative writing camp two summers in a row. Susan had been a help when I needed it, and now I was simply returning the favor.

Every sound startled. A leaf rustling. A back door opening at the other end of the alley. With every sound, with every headlight, I would stop, crouch and wait.

It was a perfect night to commit a crime. In fact, it was probably a felony if Rosie cost as much as her owner claimed. But I didn't trust him—if you had paid hundreds of dollars for a pet, why would you neglect it?

Walking down the alleyway, I made sure I was at the right house. I half remembered what kind of fence it was—from years ago—when Susan had taken me to meet Rosie, but I was a little fuzzy. What stuck in my memory most was a Beagle flying across the yard, her ears propelling like a whirligig, and baying out a love song. When she got to the end of the yard, she stuck her nose through the slats to give kisses and pressed her body against the fence to be petted. Susan was the sole source of love for this dog.

Most of what the dog knew now was sweltering heat, bitter-cold temperatures and yelled curses. When the weather got warm, there were fleas. Rosie's fur became a brown, rolling ocean of fleas. Susan offered to buy a flea collar for the dog and to even take her into the vet for treatment, but the owner refused. My friend had no other choice but to kidnap Rosie while the owner was at work, sneaking her to the vet for the flea treatment.

In the summer, there was little shade in Rosie's backyard. No one worried if the water bowl was overturned or empty. Susan would check for the owner's car and if it was gone, she would sneak into the yard and give Rosie fresh water. Come winter, the Beagle had to suffer through sleet and snow and freezing wind. Susan, when she could not stand it anymore, would bring Rosie into her own home at night, being sure to return her in the early morning before the owner noticed she was missing.

Having four dogs and a couple of cats already, Susan was not trying to fill a void when it came to Rosie. She had plenty in her four-legged family to keep her busy and feeling loved.

However, she could not tolerate any kind of cruelty toward animals. I once begged her to watch the movie *Hidalgo*; I just knew she would appreciate the Native American theme and the victory of the underdog. "No way," she told me. She knew that some of the scenes would break her heart. There were many animal movies she refused to watch, even if she knew there would be a happy ending. Susan did not foresee Rosie having a happy ending.

Getting a job offer in Boulder put Susan's emotions at war, and being able to utilize her creative potential made the position tempting. However, Colorado was a long way away from Illinois. Susan worried about who would watch out for Rosie.

Way before she had to move, Susan approached the owner with a wad of cash. "I'd like to buy Rosie, uh, Puppy. How much did you pay for her?" Sadly, the owner had never named his dog, beyond "Puppy."

The owner rattled off an amount, probably hundreds more than the truth, and then raised it a couple of times. He then said that the Beagle was not for sale. Unfortunately, later when a "For Sale" sign was stuck in Susan's yard, it cemented Rosie's fate. If Susan just took the dog with her when she moved, the owner would know what happened and might try to track her down. The thought of leaving—imagining the suffering the small dog endured and never seeing Rosie again—tore her up.

But, leave she did. The best Susan could do was stay in contact with another neighbor who reported on Rosie. And so it was for the next year and a half. Then Susan offered me a proposal: Would I help her steal Rosie? I didn't even hesitate to answer, "Yes!"

So here we were, two middle-aged women with no criminal records, who always immediately gave back extra money when a cashier made a mistake, and who never would pad the number of publishing credits to their names in order to impress editors. We were two women who were about to become thieves. Emails zipped back and forth between Susan in Colorado and me in Illinois, always in code. That's how paranoid we were. We never mentioned the dog's name or even the word "dog."

The night had finally arrived, and here I was wearing gloves (no fingerprints) and oversized boots (to leave misleading footprints), along with a hooded jacket (disguising myself as a man), standing in the alley, ready to do the dirty deed. Susan sat in my car, two blocks away, as we wanted no sighting of a Colorado license plate in the area.

Unfortunately, that evening was one of those rare nights Rosie was allowed into the house. I waited in the alley, whispered her name over and over, but soon gave up. We were both disappointed.

In the morning, I headed to work and my accomplice headed into her old neighborhood one last time. Right before lunch, the weather could not have been a better cloak—the wind picked up to almost-hurricane strength and dark clouds moved in. Rosie's owner was not home, and Rosie was out in the backyard. In desperation, Susan didn't think twice. She scooped up Rosie—who was so happy to see her—and left the gate wide-open, to make it appear that the wind had been the culprit and Rosie had run away. The two very happy and reunited souls sped away to Colorado, Rosie's soon-to-be new home.

When I checked for messages on my cell at lunch, I heard,

"The eagle has flown," which was code for a successful mission. We never knew if the old man even missed his dog. No flyers ever went up, and, as far as we knew, he didn't say a word to even one neighbor about his lost dog. So for several years Susan worried the owner might discover what really happened and have her arrested. But the owner eventually died, burying our crime with him.

Friends who now hear me tell the story are surprised. After all, does a frumpy, gray-haired woman look suspicious? Does she look like the typical felon? And Rosie? She's living the life she always deserved. Whenever I hear about the attention being lavished upon her, about the romping and playing she does with the rest of Susan's herd, I have no regrets. Ultimately, we answered to a higher power than the law.

Finding Pua's Marble

by
Jerry W. Davis, DVM

In the spring of 1969, I was stationed at Kaneohe Marine Corps Air Station, Hawaii. I was an Air Force officer on a Marine base, and my boss was a captain of the United States Navy. He was also a physician and the commander of the medical clinic on the base. Looking back at my 30 years in the military, that assignment was one of my favorites, and the following story is one of the reasons it was so special.

The captain and his wife had a Cocker Spaniel, born in Hawaii, and appropriately named "Pua," the Hawaiian word for flower! When Pua was about 6 months old, still in what I call the "puppy stage," the captain's wife called me one afternoon in a panic.

"Dr. Davis, Pua just swallowed a steel ball bearing!" she exclaimed.

"How large was the ball?" I asked.

"The size of a regular marble, perhaps a half-inch in diameter!"

"Is Pua showing any signs of discomfort or upset stomach?"

"No. She's acting like nothing happened! What can I do?!"

"We'll have to wait until tomorrow morning, X-ray Pua's abdomen and see if the bearing is passing through her intestinal tract. If it remains in her stomach, it could eventually cause inflammation. Only then can we determine a course of action," I explained.

"I'll be at your office first thing tomorrow!"

That next morning, she and Pua were waiting for me when I arrived at my office. Pua appeared normal in every way, had an appetite, and wanted to play. But there was a problem: my office was not yet totally equipped. An X-ray machine had not been installed, so I suggested to her that we take Pua off base to the nearby town of Kailua, where a civilian veterinarian could take an X-ray of Pua's abdomen. She said, "No, I'll call my husband. He's the commander of the on-base clinic and he has several X-ray machines!"

We arrived at the clinic, took Pua through a back door to the radiology section, and placed her on one of the X-ray tables. There were several human patients waiting, but Pua had priority that day. My boss made sure of that.

I took the X-ray and discovered that the ball bearing was still in the dog's stomach. I explained that if the ball remained there for a few more days, we'd have to remove it surgically. Sure enough, another X-ray two days later revealed that the ball was still in the stomach, and Pua had lost her appetite.

So there I was, a relatively inexperienced veterinarian, and my physician boss was expecting me to surgically remove a steel ball from his dog's stomach. I had not performed that particular operation before, but I was on the spot. I had no choice.

We took Pua to my office, prepared her for surgery and anesthetized her. I began the procedure, with my boss looking over my shoulder. His wife stayed at home—she couldn't stand watching her doggy undergoing surgery.

The night before, I had researched several canine surgery books on this procedure. I learned that it was sometimes difficult to locate such a small ball and extract it from the stomach. In fact, if the ball had already begun passing through the intestinal tract, it would not be found, which would make the surgery unnecessary. I made incisions through the dog's abdomen and stomach, and then searched for the steel ball. Sweat broke out on my forehead as I searched and searched, and EUREKA! I found the ball and was able to remove it, repair the incisions and Pua made a complete recovery.

Now, for the "rest of the story," as Paul Harvey would have said. The captain, having performed this procedure on humans in the past, knew, as well, that the ball might not be found in the stomach. Right after we removed Pua from the surgery table and placed her in recovery, he reached into his pocket and pulled out a steel ball bearing just like the one Pua had swallowed. He handed it to me.

"Jerry, this was just in case you were unable to find the ball. I was going to take it home and give it to my wife," he said, grinning. "Even though that wouldn't have helped Pua, my wife would have felt a whole lot better!"

Sent Packing

by
Renee Hughes

Our town of Webster Groves, Missouri, is a designated Tree City USA by the Arbor Day Foundation. It's a good thing for the dogs of our community, as thousands of outside dog urinals of all shapes and sizes offer themselves tall and proud as an opportunity for canine relief.

Not having a dog put our family in the minority. When our son joined Scouts, we determined he was old enough to appreciate a canine friend and to learn how to take care of pet. But what breed would be appropriate for our son? We decided nothing yappy, which ruled out most small dogs. Not a big barker, either. The field markedly narrowed.

One day some retired Greyhounds, walking their owners in our neighborhood, caught our attention. When your pet weighs close to 80 pounds, is substantially muscle and hits the ground running with all its might, it can top out at a speed approaching 40 mph. It walks you! Greyhounds were known to be quiet, good with children, affectionate and not big shedders. The rescue adoption groups regularly advertised how much these dogs needed good homes when they retire from racing. The socially responsible choice helped clinch the deal.

We visited the clinic that served as a halfway house for the Greyhounds transitioning from track life to a forever home. A rescue foster family had alerted us that five retired racers had been intercepted on their way to a dog-food rendering plant to be processed. Sick, but true. When we arrived at the clinic, we found ourselves surrounded by these tall, sleek, elegant animals, wrapping themselves around us like overgrown cats, with feet and tails whipping wildly. No wonder they are called "Velcro dogs."

But we were in a quandary about which one to choose. One by one, the volunteer called out each dog's name. Only one answered to his name and he did so with gusto— "Blizzard"—who was the youngest of the bunch. He was a handsome, healthy-looking brindle, and all of one and a half years old. He gazed at us with huge chestnut-colored eyes that seemed to be pleading, "Pick me!" And that was it. Love!

Blizzard had to be coaxed to navigate down steps. Common things like large trashcans, brooms and mops made him start, turn tail and hide in his crate. I could comprehend Blizzard's fear of thunder and fireworks. But I was surprised by his obvious discomfort at the high school marching band performances. He did all right with clarinets, flutes and saxophones, but when trumpets and drums joined in, he tugged so hard on his leash my wrist was bruised.

Walking with Blizzard was a fit of starts, stops, lunges,

jogs and shifts to get tangled in the leash. Alternately, I would lead and then the dog would lead. One man saw me attempting to guide Blizzard along and yelled, "Hey, you ought to try riding that thing!" A handsome dog, Blizzard elicited many requests from passersby to pet him. Blizzard's tail responded first, and then his tongue, giving his adoring admirer an impromptu bath.

Sniffing was a favorite pastime as we went by trees that must have been sporting the markings of other dogs. Blizzard was confused as to the protocol for urinating. Since rescued Greyhounds are all fixed, technically, he was an "it." He would try to raise his leg on occasion to cover the scent left on a tree. Sometimes he would be successful, other times he'd wet on himself. And on other occasions he would squat like a female. Well, he tried.

Being a rescued racer, Blizzard was, in our thinking, probably not going to be amenable to a pet rabbit that our daughter desperately wanted. We knew little about racing and thought he'd just chase a rabbit. A relative indicated that his trainers would have attached a contraption to his head with something enticing dangling out in front of him to motivate the run response. What?? We later learned Greyhounds chased a metal rabbit contraption around the track, not a real rabbit. So we consented to a rescued bunny.

The rabbit was brought home and tucked away in his over-sized cage. Blizzard tentatively approached the fenced perimeter, staring with puzzlement at this small creature. The bunny made his dislike of any sort of encroachment on his territory known immediately—stomping with loud thumps and then baring his teeth, the rabbit hissed and glared at the dog. Blizzard whined, and skedaddled rapidly to the protection of his own crate, cowering in the far back. And there you have it, a massive dog that once chased metal rabbits for training purposes was sent packing by a 5-pound bunny!

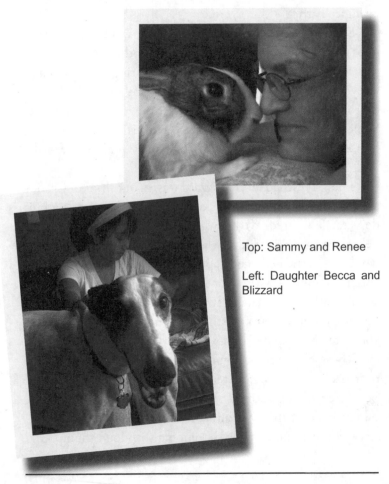

Top: Sammy and Renee

Left: Daughter Becca and Blizzard

Tale of the Little Red Dog

by
Kathy Pippig

On a late September afternoon, Gerald was out in his car. He came upon a detour, as a result of some roadwork. The alternate route forced traffic off the main thoroughfare to a smaller country road, right next to a vineyard. As Gerald drove the detour, he looked down between two rows of grapevines and something brownish-red caught his eye. Gerald slowed the car to a stop.

With a hobbling gait, a tiny animal made its way toward Gerald's car. Gerald opened his door and stepped out onto the dirt shoulder. The small animal kept advancing—its head tilted at an odd angle. As the creature drew closer, Gerald wondered how the animal could stand, let alone walk, for it was nothing but fur, skin and bones.

Gerald knelt down, keeping still, until the small dog took a few more halting steps. Then, as if surrendering, the little fur boy collapsed at Gerald's feet. He was so frail looking that Gerald hesitated to touch him. It was when the red dog turned his head up to peer at him that Gerald lost all his careful inhibition.

One of the young dog's eyes was totally destroyed. From his clear eye, the little dog studied him. He looked so sad it nearly broke Gerald's heart.

With eyes misting, Gerald gently scooped up the injured pooch. "How have you made it this far?" he muttered, while settling the little guy on the passenger seat of his car.

He drove to the vet he used for his senior Border Terrier, Chauncey. The vet, examining the dog, said, "He must be in a lot of pain with that injured eye. It has been left untreated too long."

The vet looked at Gerald, "I'll do all that I can to make him well."

Gerald nodded and left the office.

Three days later, Gerald brought the furry patient home. He had an e-collar on to prevent him from scratching at the stitches that kept his eyelid shut. The infected, damaged eye had been removed.

Gerald held the little boy and stroked him tenderly. The twinkle in the dog's remaining eye and his expression of thankful joy touched something deep in Gerald's soul. He decided to keep him, but he needed to see how his older dog would get along with the newcomer.

As it turned out, Chauncey would have nothing to do with the small red dog. There were a of couple episodes where the Border Terrier had physically threatened him. Gerald and his wife were devastated—they had both come to love their little trooper.

Therefore, Gerald called a lady who ran a no-kill shelter in the next county and asked if she might accept a little, one-eyed dog with a huge heart. She agreed readily after Gerald explained the circumstances. He added that he'd like to come by every other Friday to pick the dog up and take him home for weekend visits. It was Gerald's hope that their Border Terrier would have a change of heart and grow to accept the red dog as a friend.

One week, Gerald got a call from the lady at the no-kill shelter telling him it looked like his little rescue had found a forever home. Gerald knew the time might come when the dog, which he had never named for fear of becoming too attached, would be noticed by a loving human and taken home.

Gerald's insides twisted painfully, for this was the weekend he was to have picked the fur boy up for another try at home with the Border Terrier.

"May I come see him, one last time?" he asked.

"Of course!"

Within half an hour, Gerald was at the shelter. The lady was waiting for him, the small dog in her arms. She handed him over and the dog's tail wagged furiously as Gerald held him lovingly. Then the furry fellow showered Gerald with kisses.

Gerald hugged him tightly and murmured words of affection. He walked out to the side yard, wanting to be alone with the now-healthy fur ball, whose life he had saved. But, in saving his life, Gerald had lost his heart to a brave little warrior with a vast loving spirit.

Before he left, the lady assured him the red dog was going

to a loving home. He nodded, thanked her and drove away.

It was hard for the lady to tell him about the new home the dog was going to. She shared that it was difficult talking to a man whose heart was breaking, and hard not to cry when she looked into his eyes, which were brimming with tears.

Later that afternoon, I came to collect my new family member. I had been told the story about the little dog and Gerald. And the lady told me about the man's last visit.

In his medical files, Gerald had left a letter describing how he had come to know and love the little dog. Included in the letter was his phone number.

That night, with the phone cradled at my shoulder, I told Gerald all about the red dog's new home. I told him I had named the furry boy "Angus MacFurgus."

Gerald expressed his relief and gratitude. Then he began to tell me the tale about the courageous little dog he had rescued in the vineyard . . . which is where this story began.

Dog Detective

by
Frank Ramirez

The other day, I took our new dog Duncan out for a walk. Duncan was busy proving what I call the "Inverse Weather Dog Equation."

Just in case you played hooky the day this was introduced in math class, in layman's terms the formula is this: $2X = MW*RS$. "MW" stands for "Miserable Weather." "RS" stands for the "Right Spot," as in the spot that Duncan looks for in order to do his you-know-what duty. Simply multiply the severity of Miserable Weather times the time it takes for Duncan to find the Right Spot in order to get $2X$. The worse the weather, the longer it takes him.

As for the meaning of $2X$, I think that's pretty obvious. One of the Xs stands for the time, which is the final result of the equation. If it's bitter cold, with a wet, clingy snow falling and the wind howling, it takes Duncan much, much longer to find the Right Spot.

That other X? That stands for the words I'm muttering while I'm outside with wet feet, a cold nose and crystallized eyebrows while my glasses freeze to my face.

One of the reasons he was taking so long, I suppose, is that he was being a bit of a detective. We were out near the beehive. There are five flat stones nearby, each set into the ground. They mark the spots where, over the years, I have buried our dear departed cats, one by one. Duncan happened to sniff near a couple of the rocks, and then stuck his nose right up against the earth. He bent over, drew a deep breath, and straightened up with a startled and puzzled expression, one ear straight up and the other cocked over.

"What the heck?" he said, more or less. "What happened here?"

"That's where the cats are buried, Sherlock," I answered. That seemed to satisfy him. (Yes, my dogs and I talk to each other. No, nobody else can hear their end of the conversation. Sounds like something out of Disney, doesn't it?)

Now maybe it's in imitation of Duncan, but I've become something of a detective myself. You see, we got Duncan through TriState Collie Rescue in Indianapolis. But, I know next to nothing about him and what his life was like before he joined our family.

What I do know is they flew him from Kansas City to Indianapolis, and he didn't enjoy the flight. We picked him up in Indy and drove him to Pennsylvania, which took around eight hours. So all I know is that he was about a year old at the time we got him, and that he was from Kansas.

So what was his life like? He can't—or won't—tell me,

even though we talk to each other. It must have been pretty bad. Therefore, I've had to make some guesses.

One thing I've figured out is this—Duncan used to live around trucks. Open bed trucks. Whenever an open bed truck drives by, he gets very excited. Not the ones with a shell over the bed, mind you. They say dogs love trucks and this one is a fanatic!

The second thing is he used to live around gunshots because they don't bother him at all. Toby, our other Collie, is deathly afraid of gunshots. The first three months of Toby's life were spent on a farm owned by a pacifist Quaker woman in upstate Michigan. Nobody shoots anything there.

Not Duncan. I don't know if he was a hunting dog or not, but at the very least he was around target practice.

OK, so trucks and guns. Is this picture starting to come into focus? And there is one more clue I'd like to offer for your consideration.

First, let me say, just so you understand, I don't drink beer or anything alcoholic. But we sometimes keep a case of beer around for our guests, like our adult kids or our friends. Anyway, we'd had about half a case of Yuengling beer around the house, and our kids hadn't been able to visit for several months. Beer is not like wine. It does not get better with age. At least that's what they tell me—I wouldn't know. So the other day, my wife Jennie handed me some beer bottles. One by one I snapped them open for her and she proceeded to dump the contents down the sink.

That was clue number three. Duncan became alarmed, like someone had shot his best friend. He put his paws up on the sink and made a crying noise, watching with distress while we poured the stale beer down the drain. That made me think—not only had Duncan grown up around beer-drinking folks, but maybe someone had poured part of a bottle into his water dish. Duncan knew the smell, and I'm guessing he knew the taste.

Hmmmm, let's see. Rural Kansas. Trucks. Guns. Beer.

I'd say Duncan is a good ol' boy and used to live among a lot of good ol' boys. At this point, I wouldn't be surprised to find an iPod stuffed with country music under his blanket.

So after the last beer was dumped down the sink, I turned to Duncan and said, "Shake." He lifted up his paw and I took it in my hand.

"Hey, buddy," I said. "Welcome to Bedford County. Welcome home."

Duncan (left) and Toby

Big Red

by
Mark Crider

No home. No name. No love. Not even a ball or stuffed toy! He was just a big ol' hunk of dog I came to call "Big Red." He languished in a Corpus Christi, Texas shelter day after day, month after month, and year after year. It's not known if his first year of life was spent on the streets or if he'd been an owner surrender/throw away. However, that unwanted Labrador with red-tinged fur drew me to him like a magnet.

I visited him daily in his dark, dingy dungeon with rough concrete floor, where he was not provided even an old towel or blanket to sleep upon. Shelter workers only fed, watered and cleaned floors—they spent no time interacting with the animals. His was a pitiful existence.

Somehow Big Red remained well balanced and it was almost miraculous, considering his circumstances. He never became vicious or psychotic, although living a solitary life in confinement. My kind words and a few treats were all he received from any human. His tail wagged and I swear he smiled when he'd see me approach, calling out his name. I baby-talked, patted his head and scratched his big floppy ears while my stomach churned. There were times I thought I couldn't continue to visit the dear old fella for fear I'd end up in a straight jacket. Regardless, the next day I'd return to see my friend.

I watched Big Red change from a young dog to an aging dog. Over the course of seven years, his muzzle grayed, he developed calluses on his knees and elbows from the concrete floor, and his eyes lost some of their luster. His demeanor, however, remained the same. Food and shelter were all he expected in life—it's all he had ever known.

I wiped at tears each day when walking away and had the usual gnawing knot in my gut. Once back in my truck, I'd dig through the console for my bottle of antacids— after each visit, I ate them like they were candy.

I took numerous people to see Big Red over the years, but had no luck in finding him a home. He was too big, too old— there was always a hitch. Rescue groups passed him by thinking he wasn't adoptable. I knew I was his only hope and could never give up. I would never give up!

After all those years and all the tears I'd shed, one day the heartache suddenly turned to rage—I felt like a mad bull! I couldn't take it any longer. I was determined Big Red would have a few good years somewhere. I would not let him live and die in that damnable dungeon and time was slipping away quickly. Where had seven years gone?

I posted a plea on Facebook that evening, along with a photo of Big Red in his dungeon and added a few words about his plight.

The story went viral on the Internet and Big Red had offers of homes all across the country. At first it seemed he would be going to Georgia. Then a Houston couple—Kathryn and Jim—stepped up literally, begging for him. He'd not need to endure a long transport, only a few hours on the road headed north. Since he wasn't familiar with the outside world or cars, it was the perfect match and a short transport! I sobbed aloud with joy, even though I knew I would probably never see Big Red again. I would miss him terribly. I had come to love that dog, but it wasn't about me. It was about Big Red spending his senior years in his first real home. I felt as though the weight of the world had fallen right off my shoulders and crashed to the ground.

My grand old friend moved from a dungeon into an actual mansion, with folks who simply fell in love with his photo and his story on Facebook. As for his homecoming, the couple sent out birth announcements about that dear old Lab to friends and family.

A large dog that had never been house-trained meant for big puddles. For a period of time, he was kept on the tile floors, but Big Red had his potty habits down pat in one month's time. In wanting to please the humans that had given him a real life and love, he learned quickly.

I've stayed in touch with Kathryn and Jim. Thankfully, they understood my interest and were patient with me intruding into their lives. Without their understanding, I'd have gone crazy wondering if Big Red and his new family were adjusting to one another. I don't intend to be a pest much longer, but I had worried about Red way too many years to end up knowing nothing of his new life. I needed closure. His plight over the years was never off my mind and unknowingly I'd become a grouchy, old codger. Just ask my wife!

Big Red must have sensed he was truly wanted, for he loved everyone from day one. Well, except for the five resident cats. When he met them outside that first day at his new home, the chase was on. They scattered like greased lightning, except for a calico kitten that hung in for one lap around the pool. Then it was time to scale the fence.

With that event, Kathryn immediately had concerns about Big Red and the cats getting along. Jim assured her that Red and the cats would make their own peace, and within a week they had. The youngest cat, Max, and Big Red are now best friends and instead of playing with toys, Red prefers games of chase with his new pal. Having never had a toy, he has no interest, and probably wonders what they are—besides, a real live friend can give and share affection. He's happy to share his bed (and he has several located in various rooms) with any of the cats that choose to snuggle up close.

Kathryn and Jim attempted to rename their big boy and spent one entire evening throwing out names. Big Red would respond to none of them. He had been given a name by me, the only person that ever gave him a moment's time—he knew his name and intended to keep it.

I have learned that his days are full. Big Red loves time spent outside and lounges about the swimming pool without a care in the world. He walks three times a day and when he sees his leash, he's as excited as a young pup. He's a gentleman with each person or dog he encounters, and didn't even require being trained to walk on a leash. He just did it, and did it properly.

Jim travels and had hoped Red would be a good dog for protection. That instinct didn't surface for six weeks. On an after-dark walk one night, Big Red noticed a jogger heading toward him and his new mom—he began to growl deeply, enough so that the jogger changed direction. He now alerts to any out-of-the-ordinary sound, whether he's inside the house or outside in the yard.

Red's biggest fans seem to be his human grandparents. Jim's father calls to ask after Red more often than he inquires about his own grandchildren. Kathryn's mother has fallen head over heels as well, and spoils him terribly when she visits.

For now, Big Red's a needy dog that still can't get enough attention or petting, not even from strangers. His eyes often seem to speak, "Love me, I need you." At other times, I'm told he smiles that same kind of goofy smile that he greeted me with daily at the dog shelter.

At last, Red truly does have something worth smiling about. And I've come to realize that I'm not nearly as cranky as I was for seven long, worrisome years. It's so very simple. If Big Red is happy—I'm happy! After all, it was always about him. Mission accomplished.

Cheers, Teddy!

by
Diana M. Amadeo

When our third child was about a year old, the pressure was on to get a dog.

During spring break, I took the kids to the Humane Society. None of the pets tugged at our heartstrings. We were nearly out the door when an elderly man arrived with a tiny dog so dirty it was impossible to determine his color. The man relayed that the dog had just been retrieved from the arms of his sister—a hospice patient who had chosen to die in her home. He guessed that the Poodle was about a year old.

We asked to see the dog and found him infested with fleas. When left alone with the kids, he ran around them, over them and climbed upon them. He jumped up and planted big wet kisses on their lips. Tiring of the kids, he suddenly propelled himself up onto my chair, licked my cheek, put his head on my shoulder and fell asleep.

"What is his name?" I whispered to the old man.

"Teddy," the old man said quietly. "Sis called him that, but you can change it."

It was an impulse decision. The kids and I debated for only a few minutes. I signed papers to adopt the dirty Poodle with a promise to have him seen promptly by a veterinarian.

There was never a question that we would keep his name. When we got home, I immediately flea-dipped Teddy. He turned out to be snow white. Teddy even liked getting his teeth brushed and his hair combed. Then my husband came home from work. Oops! I forgot to let him know of our new arrival.

And so began our 15-year odyssey.

Teddy wasn't housebroken. He wasn't even tame. He wasn't a perfect dog. But his imperfections became downright endearing.

Teddy did not like being alone. There wasn't a cage that could hold him, a door he couldn't open or a lock that he couldn't figure out. On his first time alone in our home, he jumped up on my son's desk and pulled off the screen to the window. He proceeded to tear the screen to shreds.

His first Christmas with us involved his unwrapping gifts under the tree, eating the concealed chocolate and wiping his face all over my beige carpet, all before Christmas Day! When we got home that evening, he proudly brought us in to show off his handiwork. I was horrified and then relieved to find that it was only chocolate—and not what I had feared on the rug. How could such a little dog make such a profound mess?

When we had an oak staircase put in our home, Teddy somehow found his way around the barricades and left perfect doggy prints on the newly polyurethaned stairs. Our French-Canadian carpenter knew no English, but the next day cried out in exasperation, "Teddy, no, no, NO!"

About the same time we adopted Teddy, we also acquired a kitty, which was the runt of the litter. As an adult, she and Teddy were the same size. This cat had no fear. If Teddy should happen to walk by as she was dozing in the chair, out would come her paw and she would swat him in the face. The poor dog simply looked around confused. If he dared ignore her, she would meow angrily, propel herself forward and begin to chase him. Within seconds there would be a total reversal and Teddy would be chasing her. On one of these merry chases, he succeeded in toppling the Christmas tree, thus shattering some pretty expensive heirloom ornaments.

As our family grew, we added a second-story, four-season porch to our home. The contractor worked steadily for a period of time and then left it unfinished while awaiting arrival of the windows. One morning, Teddy made his way onto the porch, spied the open cutouts and took off at full speed. Like the old Mighty Dog commercial, he soared through the air before landing on the ground two floors below. Instantly, he began to cry, holding up his paw and limping. The cat sprang to the window ledge and began to meow in mockery. Teddy looked up at the cat and took off toward the house at full speed, suddenly cured.

Teddy loved the great outdoors. We went bye-bye on errands and took long, daily walks. Being so low to the ground, he got dirty easily from the road's gravel and slush. Once back home, he'd race to the kitchen sink and wait for me to hoist him up for his daily bath. His favorite part of the ritual was being wrapped in a big warm towel and cuddled like a baby.

After a severe exacerbation of multiple sclerosis, I was left relatively immobile with visual impairment and hearing loss. Teddy never left my side. He licked away my tears of self-pity and placed his paw compassionately over my weak hands. Wheelchairs and crutches followed. Teddy never left my side, smiling and wagging his tail joyously at my physical progress. Spasticity can be very painful and Teddy always seemed to know when I was in agony. He would jump up on my lap, lay his head upon my chest and give me comfort. His activity level slowed during my 10-year rehabilitation. We were inseparable. He was my shadow.

As Teddy aged, he could no longer open doors or pick locks. If my bedroom door was shut, he would lay down outside, waiting for me to awaken.

My older children went off to college and graduated. My youngest, who was a baby when we adopted Teddy, was beginning high school. He knew her routine. Everyday she'd call between 3 P.M. and 5 P.M. to be picked up from various after-school activities. As soon as the phone rang, Teddy ran to the door and waited for his sweater to be donned so we could be off for a ride.

I believe that the spirit of a living being never dies. For a week after losing Teddy, I drew comfort from the soft clinking of his dog tags.

Then I had a dream. Across from me, on a stuffed lounger, there sat Teddy. He was so human-like, with his legs crossed. In one paw he held a cigar. In the other hand was a double bourbon. He smiled and said, "It was my time anyway—don't sweat it." Then he tipped his glass in salute and was gone.

Those who know me would say that the dream was totally out of character. If I was visualizing Teddy, it would be in clouds with wings. However, in recalling his antics, the dream was Teddy. He wasn't perfect. He was silly. He didn't come off as too smart. Teddy lived his life to the fullest, his way. Now his time had come. There are no regrets.

Cheers, Teddy!

Photos from the family album

Doctor's Orders

by
Terri Tiffany

After two years of trying for a baby without success, I doubted I could endure another examination or one more office visit with three interns crowded around my lower anatomy. But my ever-faithful doctor suggested one more course of action before we gave up and spent our savings on a cruise around the world—well, maybe a cruise to the Bahamas.

"Buy a dog."

Like a dog was going to make me feel like a mother. Who was he kidding? I never owned a dog in my life. Cats were more my choice for companionship. Give me a cat any day to warm my feet in bed at night. A dog required walks and baths and trips on a leash to the vet. Not to mention the 50-pound bags of dog food that would need storage somewhere.

"It can't hurt!" My husband practically leapt out of his chair at the doctor's idea. Curt had wanted a dog since we married seven years before. I pictured a German Shepherd chasing our poor mailman down the street and receiving a bill for damages wrought.

Curt's lip drooped.

"A small one," I hesitantly agreed. I wanted a baby so badly I was willing to part with my previous prejudices.

On that very next Saturday, we found ourselves wandering through the Humane Society. Pathetic-looking creatures stretched even more pathetic-looking paws against wired pens. At the end of the last row, I stopped.

"Panda" the sign read. A white, long-haired mutt sat patiently in front of me. Her tongue rolled to the side, and one eye peeked from beneath a mound of bangs. My husband read Panda's bio. "She's 2 years old and has already delivered puppies." Even the dog had given birth. I was not totally impressed, but Curt was and asked the attendant if he could walk her.

Panda acted as if she were taking a stroll in the park. I gave her a point for good behavior, but would her presence make me pregnant? One hour and $50 later, we placed our new charge into the back seat of our Datsun and headed home, hoping we had picked the right dog.

Not five minutes on the road, we heard a retching from the back seat. I turned around and found, to my horror, Panda doubled over and heaving her lunch onto our mats.

"Stop the car!"

Curt veered off the pavement and threw open the back door. He dragged Panda to the side where she finished her deposit. Motherhood Test #1—I learned to clean up undesirables.

Test #2 took place that same night. Snuggled in our beds,

we heard the tap of toenails on our staircase. Soon, a ball of fur crept into our bedroom and slithered up onto our bed. So much for sleeping alone and getting a good night's rest.

After three weeks of dog sitting, I was convinced I knew everything I needed to know about caring for a dog. In fact, I became so absorbed in the care and upkeep of Panda that I forgot about getting pregnant.

Nine months later, I knew my doctor was a very wise man!

Speck

by
Barbara Carpenter

I didn't want another dog. When our children were growing up, we always had dogs and cats and kittens. Rather, they had us. Living on a farm offered perks like that, but a two-lane state highway ran about 200 yards in front of our house. We were fortunate to have one really smart dog, Buffy, a Poodle/ Terrier mix who survived the highway and other farm hazards for 14 years. I cried when she died, and I missed her for months. I still think about her, in fact.

I heard a very smart man remark that he didn't know what real living was until his youngest child moved away and the dog died. Now, that doesn't mean he disliked either his kid or his dog. I understood his reasoning: he was then responsible for no creature, other than himself, human or otherwise.

Our children married and gave us four grandchildren, born within an eight-year span, and we had three dogs during those years, all "pound puppies." We loved them, lost them and buried them with tears and promises to ourselves never to get another dog.

We built our dream house in a wooded area over a quarter mile behind our first house. One evening the third year of residing there beside a small lake, my husband handed a newspaper to me. It was folded to show the photo of the cutest little puppy, a Golden Retriever/Labrador mix, available at the animal shelter in a nearby town. Well, like the stupid people we are, we fell in love with the picture.

We called the shelter and made an appointment to see the pup. Short story shorter is that we brought the sweet little guy home with us, named him "Dusty" for his beautiful color, and set about learning how to live with him. It immediately became a love/hate relationship. He grew faster than we could have imagined. By the next spring, he weighed close to 100 pounds. When he jumped up—something we could not break him of doing—he was so big he could place his paws on my shoulders. This trick was not endearing, especially when I was dressed for church.

Dusty chewed and tore down the insulating strip around the garage door, and then he chewed up the wood beside it. When he started on the inside garage walls, he was demoted to a pen and a doghouse. Having him inside the house would have been disastrous. The final straw was the day he destroyed $1,500 worth of landscaping beside the deck. We decided to look for a good home for Dusty, one other than ours!

It happened quickly. Longtime friends, younger and even farther into the country, agreed to take Dusty. They fell in love with him, and the feeling was mutual. Everyone was happy.

Now we could vacation without worrying about a pet. My flowers flourished, and the house had no more canine teeth marks in the wood.

Recently, our pastor called to ask a favor. "Would you be interested in taking a dog that belongs to a sweet lady who has fallen and broken her hip?" My first thought was, *Sorry. No way.* The pastor continued. "The woman has been in the hospital for several weeks and is no longer able to care for the dog. He's been in a kennel for over a month now." *Sorry, not interested.* "The dog is a 5-year-old Chocolate Lab, housebroken, well-behaved." *Nope. Don't want any more Labs, thank you very much.* "They are running out of options."

And with his last plea, my heart dropped. I didn't want another dog—he would own me! I would be responsible for him for the rest of his life, maybe even mine. Pastor continued. "Would you and your husband just go look at the dog? His name is 'Speck.'" My heart dropped lower.

"Well, I can't promise anything, but we'll go look at the dog," I said. Big mistake.

That very evening, my husband and I went to the kennel to see this Speck. The pastor had called the kennel, alerting them to our visit, and the attendant was ready for us. She beamed as we introduced ourselves.

"Oh, you will love this dog!" she said, gushing with excitement. "He is the most lovable, polite dog we have ever had. We're all crazy about him!" *Yeah, right.* We followed her down the corridor, into the caged area. "Come, Speck!" she called.

Do you know about love at first sight? Well, both my husband and I experienced it on the spot. The most beautiful Chocolate Lab I have ever seen walked up to us, wagged his tail, licked our hands and we were lost. We looked at each other and helplessly shook our heads in defeat. We agreed to take him the next day.

From there, we went to a local farm store, and paid nearly $200 for a new doghouse, since we had given Dusty's house away. We also bought food, chew bones, and more, and then drove home as excited as two kids on Christmas Eve.

In less than a week, Speck became a part of our family, adored by our children and grandchildren. He's polite, obedient, barks only at approaching vehicles and strangers (as well as geese on the lake and howling coyotes at night), and we absolutely love him. My husband, who would never have a house dog, is now perfectly content to have Speck curled up at his feet every evening. Speck is inside the house more than he is outside, and he has yet to spend a night in the $200 doghouse outside! I kind of doubt that he ever will.

Moral: Never say never, and never underestimate the power of a Chocolate Lab's warm brown eyes. No doubt, heartbreak is out there for us in the future somewhere. But for now, we have the sweetest Speck you can imagine in our home.

Barbara and Speck

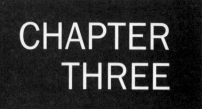

CHAPTER THREE

Companions Like None Other

Love and loyalty know no boundaries.

Love Bites

by

Ken McKowen

It wasn't long after we purchased our new home in a rural neighborhood that our family decided we needed a dog. After all, we reasoned, everyone who lived on an acre of land should have animals of one kind or another.

Locating a rescue organization, we went to see two puppies that were sisters, although they didn't look anything alike. Both different colors, the pups were Vizsla/Lab/Rhodesian Ridgeback mixes, and we were assured they wouldn't get bigger than 60 pounds. Rather than taking only one puppy and leaving the other an abandoned psychotic mess, we adopted both puppies and took them home. My wife, Dahlynn, reasoned that a single dog would become too lonely whenever we traveled, as back then we were full-time travel writers.

Dahlynn's young daughter claimed the bigger, light-brown puppy and named her Shilo. Her younger son, Shawn, latched onto the smaller, dark-brown puppy and she became Coco. Shilo immediately set herself up as the dominant member of the two-dog pack, with Coco happily following behind. Both of our spayed girls greatly surpassed the promised 60 pounds of dog; fully grown, Coco weighed in at 75 pounds and Shilo tipped the scales at nearly 100 pounds.

When Shawn turned 12, he asked for another pet, and that's when Fred came home from the pet store. Fred was a boy parakeet, or boy budgie is probably more accurate, although I have no idea what separates one species of bird from the other. They all looked the same, only different colors. Fred was green.

On the day Fred came home to live with us, we placed his cage on a small, low table in front of a long wall of windows that faced out over our parcel of land. The dogs were out back, but they sensed something exciting going on inside the house. When we let them in, they headed immediately to Fred's cage. They were very excited, plastering their noses against the wire bird jail! They sniffed, licked and snorted around the cage— and slimed the hardwood floor arond the cage with their constant flow of slobber. At first, Fred freaked with all the unexpected canine attention, but within a few days he figured out he had nothing to fear, enjoying the safety of his cage.

Both dogs continued to spend hours with their noses pressed tightly against Fred's cage, whining, crying, licking, and jumping from side to side every time the bird changed positions. Shilo was the most demented. Coco would tire of the focused attention after an hour or two and go lie down, quietly awaiting some type of extraordinary noise from Shilo or Fred—a signal to rejoin the vigilant bird watching. It didn't take long for Fred to become quite comfortable with the two dogs' noses constantly pressed firmly against his cage. Fred often perched himself on the cage bars and pecked at the dogs' nose whiskers, which simply excited them even more.

Shilo and Coco's antics served as humorous entertainment for our family and for our many visitors and houseguests. It was the most bizarre dog behavior we had ever witnessed. Some suggested we video the threesome and submit it to the funniest video television program, but we never did, opting to keep their escapades out of the limelight. After a couple of years, the dogs settled down somewhat. At least the floor became less likely to be covered with dog slobber, although the perpetually scattered birdseed was another matter. Shilo still pressed her nose to the cage and Fred would "kiss" her; Coco became ambivalent, only rarely displaying her old, bird-brained craziness.

Dahlynn and I often discussed Shilo's continued attentiveness toward Fred, and smiled over this unique friendship. The two were inseparable as Shilo always had one eye on Fred. If we walked from the living room to the dining room, Shilo jumped up and kept herself between us and the bird. The little parakeet continued to groom Shilo from within his cage and squawked whenever her canine companion wandered off, even for a moment. This always brought Shilo running back, full speed, to check on her feathered friend. Fred had her trained!

Alas, we came home one day to find Fred dead, claws-up, on the bottom of his cage. We put Fred on ice, so to speak, placing him in a small box in the freezer, awaiting a proper burial. Shilo was upset to see the empty birdcage and looked all over the house for Fred. Eventually, she dropped to the floor and slept. She was depressed, so we gave her extra pets and cried right along with our old Shilo girl.

On the day we gathered for the avian funeral, I carried Fred's little coffin from the freezer to the backyard. Shilo must have sensed I had Fred, and she came over to me, whining. Dahlynn suggested I let Shilo sniff a proper dog goodbye to her dear friend, so I opened the box and lowered it to Shilo's nose level. Shilo hesitated for perhaps a tenth of a second before lunging at the bird, taking the entire tiny frozen, feathery friend into her mouth. Dahlynn screamed as I pried the bird from Shilo's locked jaws, before Dead Fred could become Fed Fred. I succeeded in retrieving the broken budgie, feathers slightly askew. Shilo sat with a look of total satisfaction on her face.

We buried Fred in our patio garden, comforted with the knowledge that Shilo really did miss little Fred—in more ways than we had ever thought possible.

Fred, Coco and Shilo

Jake

by
Glady Martin

For most of my adult life, I have had problems fitting in with new people. Shy by nature, I have never been part of a clique or even a pack, to use a dog term as an example. But everything changed when I met Jake and his human parents, and several of their friends, as well. We hit it off wonderfully—that is, I found great human friends. But big dogs scared me, including Jake.

Jake was a large Akita Shepherd. He may not have been very tall, but the size of his head made up for it. His parents owned an auto-recycling business and Jake fit right in; he knew it was his domain and he was on constant guard duty. Many people felt uncomfortable when they saw the massive-headed hound. Jake looked fierce indeed, which was the main reason I feared him.

Jake's parents had a beautiful two-story home built to

order. There were boundaries in the home that Jack could not breach, and he knew and honored those confines. On occasion, Jake was allowed into the television room when the family was watching a movie, but he wasn't allowed anywhere else in the home that was carpeted. Since the kitchen floor was ceramic tile, Jake was allowed in there, and he loved it, especially when it was treat time.

Again, I was deeply afraid of Jake. I always stiffened up when his dad would bring him into the kitchen so Jake could perform tricks for friends and family. My fear was so bad that I could hardly breathe. I had heard that animals sense when you're afraid, but even in my silent terror, I was intrigued by the obedience of this short but mighty canine.

For one of the tricks, his master placed a big piece of meat on Jake's nose, turned away and took his time before he whispered, "OK." Jake would immediately throw the meat up into the air with his nose and catch it in his huge mouth, exposing even bigger teeth. More often than not, the meat was swallowed whole. I wondered if he even tasted it. Maybe anticipating the wait caused him not to care about the taste, because waiting was the name of the game—not the food itself.

No matter how many times I witnessed Jake's talent, I was always amazed. Jake's dad and pack leader then decided to take his training further by piling two pieces of meat on his nose. It was quite incredible to see this dog sitting as still as a rock, the only movement being the saliva dripping from his anxious mouth. His eyes looked straight ahead, not daring to move. Once again, when the magic word was whispered, Jake would throw both pieces up and catch them in a fraction of a second.

One long weekend, my new group of friends and I went camping along a nearby river. At the time, I was experiencing back trouble and begged off joining an organized ride on some four-wheeler quads brought along on the trip. Another friend and I chose to stay behind in camp and do some reading instead.

Later that day, I went for a walk alone along the riverbank. Not far into my stroll, I felt fur around my legs. *Oh, my gosh! It's Jake!* I thought in terror. And it was. Suddenly, Jake let out a low, long growl from his barreled chest, one that shook me to my core. I instantly froze, afraid to move one muscle. I was sure I'd never make it back to camp. I thought quickly, *If he attacks, I'll throw myself over the bank and into the river.*

Jake's growling became louder and more persistent. Again, I stood completely still, afraid to move, and the bitter taste of fear formed in my dry mouth. I then heard behind me a fearful male voice yelling, "Call off your dog! Call off your dog!"

Like a lightning bolt, I realized Jake was protecting me! I turned slowly to face a man I had never seen before. He had a beer in one hand, bright red eyes and a leather whip attached to his belt! All I could say was, "I can't call him off. He's not my dog!" The man backed up slowly and disappeared.

It took several moments before I realized what had just occurred. I fell to my knees crying and wrapped my arms around Jake's thick neck, thanking him over and over again. He whimpered like a little puppy and left wet lick marks all over my face, but I didn't care. Jake was my hero!

Since that day, whenever Jake sees me from a distance when riding in the back of his master's truck, it takes all the obedience he has to stay in that truck until it comes to a stop. Then the greeting begins! After all the licking and whining are over, Jake leans his massive body against mine, which in dog language means, "I trust you and will protect you because you are a part of my pack." I know that because I looked it up in a dog-language book.

I feel proud and honored that I have been made a part of the pack by this awesome canine friend. With Jake's love, I have been able to get past my fear of dogs. Thank you, Jake. You will forever be in my heart, forever in my memories and forever within this story.

Jake with Glady's brother Randy

Treasures of Old

by
Angela Walker

A couple of Houston Collie Rescue volunteers transported a sad, senior, heartworm-positive Collie that had been sent to a kill shelter by his owners. They named him "Desperado," a very fitting name considering his plight.

I sent out a plea to our volunteers, asking if anyone could please foster this dear old man. Like most rescue groups, our foster homes were bursting at the seams, some doubled and tripled up on fosters. We had no choice but to place him at a boarding kennel until a foster home was available.

A few days passed and I just couldn't shake the thought that he was in boarding. My roommate and I discussed it and decided he should be sprung from that environment. When I picked him up from the kennel, he bounded out of there like he knew he was going home.

Desperado was skin and bones. It was going to require much

care for him to become a healthy boy again. We began his path back to good health immediately, in fact that very evening.

My friend, who is also a groomer, had no choice but to shave him because he was so terribly matted. It was much less stressful than trying to comb or brush out the enormous amount of tangled, knotted and dirty hair. We worked slowly, took breaks and gave him treats to reassure him we only wanted to help. We began at 8:30 P.M. and finished at 11 P.M. that first evening. He had skin sores behind some of the mats that never would have healed, but only become worse without attention. I'm sure he slept more peacefully that night than he had in months, maybe years.

Desperado made his debut in the world by hanging out at the Houston Collie Rescue booth and meeting his adoring public (he was positive they adored him) at the 2010 Reliant Dog Show. Like so many Collies, he had a lot to say as he barked his way through Reliant. He barked at everyone who passed by unless they stopped to pet him. I wondered if he were looking for his family.

That fall, I decided he was home after all and named him "Runner." My home was his home! He turned out to be the perfect dog and loved all people. He was also the textbook example of a therapy dog. Once he regained his health, we went to work on training. He had the handshake mastered, and, in fact, could be found standing in front of my recliner, continually lifting his paw for a shake. The old saying, "You can't teach an old dog new tricks," is so incorrect! Furthermore, he then passed his Good Canine Citizenship test and became a certified therapy dog. He has brought much love and happiness to the lonely or forgotten senior citizens who reside in assisted living or nursing homes in our area.

When Runner's not working, he spends his time hanging out with his feathered friends. Last spring, we obtained some baby chicks from the feed store. Runner was captivated by them. He allowed the tiny babes to play around him, upon him, climb over him and even to nestle up close in his thick, dense coat to nap. And this past spring, we purchased our very first duckling. Runner was just as enamored with the duckling as he was with the chicks. When his bird friends were out in the afternoons, he could be found lying in the yard with them or following them about as he attempted to keep them out of harm's way.

To this day, I am not sure why Runner was turned in to a horrid kill shelter. It is so true what they say: "One man's trash is another man's treasure." That 12-year-old, sickly senior dog became so much more and has brought much joy to everyone and everything he encounters. It just doesn't get any better than that, for man or dog or feathered friends galore!

Runner with a chick

From Rags to Riches

by

Pat Wahler

Our family lived in the country, where raccoons, fat squirrels and possums populated the woods. Unfortunately, so did dogs. Some belonged to neighbors and some were wanderers, either abandoned or lost. The sight of a dog padding down the road or seeking a handout always broke my 12-year-old heart. So any time a willing stray appeared, I'd coax it to my house, hoping it might stay and become my own.

Mom and Dad did not approve. They told me I wasn't ready for the responsibility of a pet. Then, as though in agreement, each of my rescues would mysteriously disappear. Any questions on what happened always got the same response. Dad rattled the newspaper in front of his face while Mom gave her standard reply, "He (or she) must have gone home."

As with any fairy story, I didn't quite believe it. It seemed far too unlikely that whenever a dog entered my life, it suddenly gained such a sharp sense of direction. I suspected my parents had an under-the-table arrangement with the dog catcher, but I couldn't prove a thing. Yet the fact remained—no dog ever stayed as more than a transient visitor.

It wasn't a surprise the day I found my latest potential canine companion. He resembled a middle-aged, short-legged, long-bodied, Hound-dog mix. Small but mighty, he bore the marks of a dubious past with the swaggering bravado of a prizefighter. No lowered tail or sad eyes. He seemed to have the heart of a scruffy champion, if not the pedigree.

He trotted over to me when I whistled and swallowed the crumbled cookies produced from my pocket. Treats always enticed a hungry dog to follow where I led and this one was no exception. We became better acquainted as we walked. All dogs needed a name, so I decided to call this one "Rags," after the canine hero of a story I'd read. The name fit his unkempt exterior like a worn leather glove.

Once we arrived home, I introduced Rags to my parents. They exchanged a resigned look as he thumped his tail politely in greeting. I snatched some lunchmeat from the refrigerator and brought it to him. He ate it like a gentleman, and then found a spot of dappled shade under our pine tree. I crossed my fingers and hoped this time my house would be more than a doggy one-night stand.

The next morning, I ran outside with a plate of breakfast scraps. Rags sat on the front porch as though waiting for me. He gobbled down every bite and then drank straight from the streaming garden hose without a qualm. Nothing bothered Rags. He seemed to me the epitome of canine perfection.

I scratched his ears until the sound of footsteps on gravel

turned my head. I saw Grandma walking toward our house to visit Mom, as she did nearly every day. Alarm flickered in my stomach—Grandma lived in terror of dogs. Dad told me that as a child, she'd been badly bitten by a stray, fostering a lifelong fear. Whenever a dog came near, she'd either freeze or scurry away. And since Grandma walked far more often than she drove, her phobia created problems.

In those days, leash laws didn't exist. Both claimed dogs and castaways ran free. Grandma had several unpleasant encounters with them. Dogs seemed to sense her fear, raising hackles and barking a challenge whenever their paths crossed.

I strolled toward Grandma, hoping Rags would stay put. Instead, he ambled along behind me, tail swishing amiably. Even I recognized the sharp pinch of fear in her face. I stopped walking and Rags sat down beside me, his tongue dripping from an already steamy morning.

Grandma lifted her hand in greeting and hurried past us into the house. I shrugged and forgot about her, far more interested in checking Rags for ticks, the plague of all country dogs. He watched me, mildly tolerant to my pokes and prods.

It wasn't much later when Grandma reappeared outside. She mumbled goodbye and shot a sideways glance toward Rags before hurrying away with a steady stride. I watched her and wondered if she'd complained to Mom about Rags. I frowned at how that might affect my plans. Then the sound of Mom's voice cut through the summer air.

"Patty! Come in and clean your room."

I complained bitterly to Rags, who listened with his head angled to the side. Why did I have to go in when there were so many better things to do outside? My feet dragged until Mom called again. Fear of swift retribution spurred me inside to make my bed and gather scattered treasures. Once my labors passed inspection, Mom released me from further duties. I grabbed a hairbrush from the dresser. Rags' coat could use some sprucing up.

Outside, my bare feet danced on the hot concrete of the sidewalk while I looked one way and then the other. Rags had disappeared.

I raced back inside to find Mom on her knees scrubbing the kitchen linoleum.

"Where's Rags?"

She looked up only long enough to answer.

"I don't know. Maybe he went home."

Despite my mother's maddening lack of concern, I ran outside and launched an all-points search on the dusty roads near our house. I looked for Rags until the air began to cool and shadows lengthened. Nothing! Finally I trudged home and wondered what sort of strange direct hotline my parents had developed with the dogcatcher.

That evening we sat down for dinner. My sister stuffed her baby cheeks full of mashed potatoes while I pushed my food around and pouted. Only the sound of forks on plates could be heard until the telephone sounded a shrill jangle. Dad got up to take the call. For once, I didn't even try to eavesdrop.

A few minutes later, he returned to the table. Mom looked up with her fork poised midair.

"Who was that?"

Dad picked up his napkin. Then he looked at me.

"Grandma called. It seems Rags followed her home."

Mom's fork clattered to the table.

"What? She must have been terrified."

"She tried to shoo him away at first, but he stayed right on her heels until that big brown dog of the Johnson's came rushing toward them. Grandma said she heard a growl just before Rags tore after the other dog and chased him away. Then he trotted back and walked with her all the way home."

My mouth popped open in a fly-swallowing "O."

"She says it's the first time she felt safe from the neighborhood dogs. So when they got to the house, she gave him a soup bone to chew. She'd like to know if we could spare Rags to walk with her every day."

My eyes must have been bigger than two homegrown cantaloupes. Could Dad mean what I hoped he meant?

"You've been pretty responsible with your chores lately. I guess you could handle taking care of a dog. Especially one your Grandma likes to have around."

My grin strung from one ear to the other. Mom rolled her eyes and let me run to the window. There sat Rags, canine hero and future Grandmother escort, waiting on the porch. He may not have had a pedigree, but I knew that dog had the heart of a champion.

No one objected when I grabbed a fistful of meatloaf before running outside. Rags gobbled down the food and licked my fingers clean. I threw an arm around his neck and felt his warm little body lean into mine. With Grandma on my side, I wasn't worried about any treachery between my parents and the pound.

And that's the way one little dog named Rags finally

earned a permanent place in my home . . . and my heart.

Pat holding Rags, with younger sister Barb

Flat on My Back with a Flat

by
James M. Pearson

I broke my neck in a diving accident at 26 years of age. My injury left me a quadriplegic, although I had very slight use of some muscle in both lower arms and hands. There are different levels of quadriplegia—some quads can't breathe on their own or move one muscle. I felt fortunate that I could hold a can of cola, very awkwardly, but at least I could do it! Always being an independent soul, I felt no need for a service dog and certainly could not afford one.

Yes, there were times I needed help and had no way to ask for it if I couldn't get to a telephone—that happened numerous times when I fell out of my wheelchair. I was fortunate that friends and family kept close tabs on me. I required someone to transfer me from my wheelchair into bed each night, and assistance getting out of bed, showering and dressing in the morning. When I did find myself in a hopeless situation, I always knew that within at least 12 hours, help would arrive.

Many years after my accident, friends had been secretly working together to improve the quality of my life. At the end of a nice weekend visit with one of those friends, I was handed a stack of forms to fill out. They had raised enough money to get me a service dog! I was speechless, to say the least. With all red tape completed, I found myself on a plane to California, and it was a flight that would change my life forever.

In California, I met my new canine companion—"El Pomar." A yellow Lab, El Pomar came by way of CCI (Canine Companions for Independence). The two of us bonded immediately—we were a perfect match. After our training, which included El Pomar mastering 45 commands that would specifically help me, we both proudly graduated from CCI. Over the next two years, several more commands were added, many to help me become more independent, and others just for fun! You know, like Pomar (my nickname for him) putting his paw over his face when I would ask, "Who farted?"

By the time my faithful companion retired to spend the rest of his life just being my best buddy, El Pomar knew approximately 200 commands. Some of them emerged as we did agility together, such as learning to "Tunnel" or "Over" and so forth. Many commands were learned for demonstrations I did with Pomar. We often went to a library, school or church to demonstrate how a service dog works. I could always count on keeping people's attention by throwing Pomar a funny and unexpected command like the "Who farted?" gag.

During his time with me, I taught Pomar basic commands for emergency situations. He knew how to dial 911 and bark into the phone. I taught him on a phone designed for people with hearing and sight difficulties. It had a large keyboard and I programmed every key to 911. Thus, I could give El Pomar his cue, which was "Gency"—short for "emergency." He'd go to the telephone, knock the receiver off the hook, hit one of the keys with his paw and bark into the telephone. The 911 operators in my town of Colorado Springs, Colorado, had been forewarned that if they ever heard a dog barking from my phone number, I needed help.

Unfortunately, I was complacent in having the phone where El Pomar could always find it. In such cases, I gave him the "Phone" command. He'd retrieve the nearest telephone, bring it to me, and I'd call for help. It came in handy many times. I always seemed to find ways to fall out of the wheelchair, turn it over, or discover myself in some sort of ridiculous predicament. I think Pomar thought it was a game. In truth, I did try to make his commands seem like a game—I wanted him to enjoy his work as much as I appreciated it.

Once, when doing laundry, I wasn't aware that I'd run over a carpet tack and had one tire that was as flat as a pancake. With a flat, any wheelchair becomes tipsy. Coming out of the laundry room, I usually placed my hands on each side of the doorway to give myself a big pull to roll out fast. Yep, I like to go fast whenever possible. However, with a flat tire, when you pull hard, the front wheels tend to rise upward. Naturally, I went over backwards. There I was, flat on my back in the laundry room, looking at a wheelchair several feet away.

My chair was blocking the door, so Pomar could not even get in. It happened to be a day when I'd left up on the bookshelf the large phone he could use. Pomar brought me a cordless phone after I gave the "Phone" command. I cannot explain how he managed to get around the wheelchair blocking the door to the utility room. Jumping was not an option with me on the floor—he'd have landed right on top of me. Still, he somehow found a way to maneuver around me and the wreckage with a phone in his mouth.

I needed to be on my side to dial the phone, which was impossible. However, I could get just far enough over that I used my tongue to hit 911. I tried explaining to the operator how a grown man could find a way to flip his wheelchair over inside his house, have his dog bring the phone and call for help. Of course, the person wanted to know if I was OK. Overall I was, except for my pride. I apologized for calling the emergency number instead of the fire department. "No problem," the operator said, and she would not let me hang up until help arrived.

I'm only a few miles from the fire station and within minutes, I heard sirens. Keep in mind, nothing was wrong with me other than me being out of my wheelchair, not a bruise— nothing except my wounded pride. Still, there I lay with my faithful dog, a phone by my side and the wheelchair just feet from me—but it might as well have been a mile!

Bill, a deacon in our church, was also captain of the Colorado Springs Fire Department, in charge of the hazmat squad. He'd been scanning his Fire Department radio and saw the call from my house. Soon there was a fire truck, ambulance, two police cars, Captain Bill and his hazmat team in my house! I'm guessing 12 to 15 people in all. I wanted to crawl into a hole.

I was examined while still on the floor, and after they all determined I was fine, they said it was OK to help me back into my chair. But before doing so, they had to fix the flat. I had an extra wheel, so the fellas took care of tire change. While I waited, I so wanted to get up, get the gaggle of people out of my house and find a way to heal my wounded pride. Oh, but Captain Bill had other thoughts.

"Wait, don't you guys get him up yet! I want you to see something!"

Captain Bill asked me if I could tell Pomar to get a Coke from the refrigerator. I agreed, because I would do anything to get off that floor. I said the magic word, "Coke." Pomar jumped over the wheelchair, trotted to the refrigerator, opened the door, got me a Coke, brought it back and waited for me to take it from his mouth. Of course, that was impossible in my situation, being on the floor. I asked him to "Drop It" instead and he complied. He returned to close the refrigerator door and waited for me to play ball with him. His favorite reward following any command was to play ball.

But wait—Captain Bill had more things he wanted to show the guys. I decided I had to end this nonstop sideshow and decided to bargain with El Pomar's skills.

"You get me up and I'll show you a trick," I bartered. Before I knew it, I was back in my chair.

Pomar demonstrated many things for the crew that day, from turning light switches on and off to retrieving everything from a dime to a 10-pound weight. He took several bows—well deserved, I might add—and performed "Who Farted?" at least a dozen times. Trust me, he played a lot of ball that day and received much extra love from a bunch of great guys who were there only to help. Thanks to Captain Bill, the gang ended up watching a 30-minute doggy show, but I don't think one of them minded at all!

Once again, El Pomar was the star. If not for his skills, I might be telling you this story from the laundry room floor instead of sitting at my computer, pride restored, sharing awesome memories of my service dog and hero. In our years together, we made more new friends and placed smiles on more faces than I can count. But most importantly, my faithful buddy El Pomar made my life complete.

Note: James "Jim" Pearson unexpectedly passed away after submitting his story. A champion of man's best friend, Jim left a lasting legacy for canines everywhere. As such, this book has been dedicated to him.

~~ Kathleene Baker

El Pomar, Jim and
wife Serena

We Danced

by
Patricia Frank

Simon came into this world on the first day of a brand new year, just over seven years ago. Little did I know what was in store for both of us when he became my critter kid!

Even though much of my time was given to other members of our critter herd, Simon and I found a shared love for something we both totally enjoyed, just the two of us together—an unimaginable partnership that evolved both on and off the agility course. Only those who have experienced life with an agility dog can truly understand that relationship. During the hours and hours of training and learning together, we grew to know each other so well that we could read each other's thoughts.

I was so proud of Simon when he mastered the commands of "Left" and "Right" on the agility course. He seemed to easily and willingly absorb what I needed from him as a partner. More than once, he anticipated the right move on the course, while

I contemplated the wrong one. All spectators were amazed at how high Simon soared over the course jumps. From the very beginning, I was in awe of his mastery of all course obstacles with such precision and speed. By running a competition course perfectly, in under half of the judge's course time, Simon truly showed everyone how it's done.

And Simon added great humor to some of our course runs. I'm not sure I felt like smiling, however, when he'd leave me to go bark at the judge. But, he always picked up where he left off to finish the run with style, and still under the allotted time limit. Simon was a crazy clown doing serious work—like when he entered the wrong end of a curved tunnel, somehow managed to turn his big body around while still inside, exited and then re-entered at the correct end. And once he fell off the high boardwalk, landing atop the tunnel obstacle underneath with just one foot. Not missing a beat in his gait, he continued on the course.

I guess that I shouldn't have been so surprised at our success. When I first saw Simon as a pup, I knew he had what it took to enjoy agility. Two dogs before him shared the sport with me, and my not-so-novice eye saw the agile manner in his play. His obedient response to my command of "Come" was instantaneous—even when running after a squirrel that had challenged him to a game of chase! To my agility eye, he was more than impressive. He turned on a dime when called to return, leaving the squirrel relieved, I'm sure! His abundant energy never allowed him to tire. Simon was constantly upbeat, charming, yet filled with rambunctiousness, especially as a young dude.

After about a year and a half of weekly training classes and hours of practice at home on our own agility obstacles, we became one on the course. When it was time to enter our first trial, however, I believe Simon and our training-class instructor had more confidence than I did. With my inability to keep up with him, I thought he'd find the excitement too much at only 2 years of age, and go overboard with enthusiasm. I asked for us to be entered in the lowest level—Level 1. Our trainer laughed and said we needed to be entered in Level 2, where we would be required to do the set of six weave poles. Yes, the other dogs would be more experienced. Simon didn't seem to be nervous about the idea, though, so I took a deep breath and signed us up.

Simon shone in the ring and on his very first time in a sanctioned trial, he received a qualifying run toward his jumper's title. He also placed first in his class with the best course time and had no faults. Simon gracefully soared over those jumps, bounding several inches higher than the required 24 inches for his height, where the bar was set. In addition, he did it all with a smile on his Poodle face.

I will always remember the agility trial we attended in Williamston, Michigan. Simon's "dad" and I readied our little camping site near the agility rings. We parked our van and set up our screened awning near its tailgate. After registering, we unloaded the cooler, lawn chairs and dog supplies. We were very well organized by the time Simon and I were to go in the ring for our first run.

As always, I went into the ring beforehand for the judge's meeting with all those participating in that division. Dad took

Simon on-leash to wait until I got back. However, Simon seemed to have forgotten that dogs cannot attend the judge's meeting. After receiving the judge's instructions, participants were walking the course and planning strategies when I heard someone say, "It's the Poodle."

I didn't pay much attention even when someone else said, "Yes, it's the Standard Poodle."

I must say that I did react to the loudspeaker when the voice said, "His name is Simon, and he's running loose! Please get your dog!"

Needless to say, I scooted out of the ring and met Simon, carrying his own leash, running down the course aisle lickety-split. I thought perhaps he was upset that I had forgotten him and wanted to make sure I didn't run the agility course alone!

We ventured back to our campsite and found Dad dozing in his chair, his leash-holding hand relaxed, totally unaware that he had failed in his responsibility of watching over Simon. Thus, Simon had taken off in pursuit of some fun and adventure.

Fortunately, Simon never slept on the job. However, knowing him as an independent creature, I wouldn't have put it past him to stop in at his favorite agility obstacle—the tunnel—where it was shady and cool, to take a brief snooze before finishing the course. Luckily, the cliché, "Like father, like 'critter' son," never did apply!

Simon was a constant instigator of fun and mischief and used every waking moment enjoying life. His upbeat attitude and energies sometimes got him in trouble, but he added zest to my life and provided smiles for my face. With great jubilance, he was always prancing throughout our home with that ever-so-regal and elegant Standard Poodle stride, even after being naughty and told to go to his room. That joyful attitude of his made me feel younger and gave me motivation to reach for the stars. At this stage in my life, I'm trying so hard to grow old gracefully and he made it easier for me to do that. Simon left an indelible Poodle-mark on my existence that affected my whole being.

Thank you, Simon, for our dance together. During all of the amazing moments we shared, the world was so right . . . our lives so full of fun . . . creating the wonderful memories that will be stored forever in my heart! Although our dance is over, you will be forever cherished.

Simon and Patricia's granddaughter Olivia

Trusting Tanner

by
Rebecca Kragnes

Up until age 24, I was frightened of most animals, and especially dogs. The fur of a dog felt wonderful, but a shift in position could reveal potentially harmful paws and mouths.

This may not have affected someone who could see the dog was about to move, but I have been blind since birth. If I were stroking a dog's silky back and it suddenly turned its head, my next stroke could land upon a wet mouth filled with sharp teeth. That unexpected change in texture was startling to me. Licking was revolting, and where there was a tongue, there were teeth! I was also skeptical that animals were capable of emotion and empathy. My negative feelings about animals gradually turned to love after meeting my first Seeing Eye dog—a Golden Retriever named "Tanner."

My fiancé, Phil, had a German Shepherd guide dog named "Andy." Andy didn't have a mean bone in his body. However, he was also vocal, had rough fur and was prone to skin allergies which produced an unpleasant odor. During my visits to see Phil, and prior to Tanner coming into my life, I walked with him and Andy to get a feel for how a guide dog worked. For example, snowdrifts always disoriented me, but Andy handled them beautifully. It was also amazing to me that Andy had also learned "intelligent disobedience." If Phil gave Andy a "Forward" command, Andy would disobey if he saw something which didn't look safe.

By spending this time with Andy, I learned the advantages of traveling with a dog, but knew that love had to be part of the equation for a real working partnership. Because of my fear, I didn't know if I could ever love a dog. But Phil strongly encouraged me to apply for a dog. He reassured me that if it didn't work out, I'd come home without one. Phil later admitted that he suspected all along that I'd fall in love.

In June 1996, I went to The Seeing Eye in Morristown, New Jersey for training. I told my instructor my feelings and described the things I didn't like about Andy. When Tanner came to me, my instructor warned me that Tanner licked, but he promised we would work on that. Tanner's fur was silky soft and he was still, quiet and had been bathed and sprayed with wonderful doggy cologne. It seemed my trainer had thought of every possible negative to eliminate for our first encounter.

"OK," I said in a tremulous voice directed to my new canine acquaintance, "You can lick me."

During our training, poor Tanner had to endure a few days of me putting the harness on incorrectly. One time I was so frustrated by the harness that I started to cry. Tanner stood very still, as if to say, "Try again. I'll be patient." Then he gently licked my tears.

Tanner's lick wasn't revolting, and I learned about his empathy. By the end of the second week, I was no longer washing my hands after every lick, and even though I knew praising him by saying, "Good boy," resulted in more licks, I did it anyway.

As we bonded, our work kept improving. Then the day came that my instructor insisted I go to New York City with Tanner. I was about to move to Minneapolis, a large city, and it was decided that if I could get around New York comfortably with Tanner, I would have no hesitation when I moved. Despite my terror of walking in New York City, Tanner was the Crowd King! He adroitly got me around big crowds that I would have had to plow through with a cane. I had never felt such exhilaration.

At the beginning of training, I was scared to trust Tanner. By the end, Tanner proved himself to be a capable guide in all diverse situations. But there was one more big fear to overcome during our first couple of years together—I was afraid of growling, barking dogs in close proximity. That fear traveled down the leash and Tanner felt he had to be more protective. He started barking and growling back, which in turn made me afraid of Tanner. After a couple of unpleasant encounters with other dog handlers, an instructor helped me break the cycle of fear, assuring me that Tanner would never hurt me. Once I wasn't afraid of Tanner, I was finally able to comfortably put my life in his paws when traveling.

Through our partnership, Tanner gave me many gifts by teaching me that I could bond with him, trust him and know that he and other animals had emotions. This knowledge transferred into my other partnerships. I'm so grateful for all that my beloved Tanner taught me.

Side by Side

by
Mark Crider

My grandmother, whom everyone called Katie, was widowed very young and left to raise three small children on her own. It was a difficult task and she worried day in and day out, especially one year, with colder weather right around the corner. Because the family's food was almost non-existent and with the holidays fast approaching, Katie contemplated asking once again for more credit at the only store in town—the mine store.

The mine, owned by Boyce Thompson, employed nearly the entire population of Superior, Arizona, including my grandfather before his untimely death. Most miners were never debt-free. Pay often didn't cover essential expenses from one check to the next. Thus, their only choice was to buy food on credit from the mine store.

By December, Katie's food allotment was down to bare

bones. Not to mention, she had not been able to skimp and hoard away anything for a Christmas dinner. She so wanted to have something special for her children, since there would be no gifts. But she had only the staples to make biscuits and gravy almost daily. There had been absolutely nothing to hoard away.

A friendly, young, female dog had shown up late in November that year. It took several days before she was comfortable enough to begin lounging on the rickety, old wooden porch. She had wavy, rust-colored fur, warm brown eyes, floppy ears and a fluffy tail. A mere mutt, it was impossible to tell what her parents might have been. Still, she was a pretty girl and she watched Katie's every move. When the two made eye contact, her tail wagged briskly, although she kept her distance. The dog seemed very cautious, but Katie figured eventually they would become friends, for the stray had already become friends with her children.

"I wonder why she's staying here with me and the kids," Katie mumbled to herself, while sitting on the sunny porch with the dog. "And why hasn't she lost weight since we haven't been able to share one scrap of food? It's a mystery, but she's finding something to eat somewhere."

Katie got up and went inside the tiny ramshackle house to fix biscuits and gravy for supper, yet again. Her children would be home soon. They trudged over five miles each morning and evening to attend school in town, and were ravenous by supper time.

Soon Katie saw the children coming up the dirt road to the shack. The dog was prancing alongside them with her tail a-wagging.

"What has that dog got in its mouth? It looks like a rabbit. Oh . . . it is a rabbit! We'll have dumplings instead of biscuits and gravy tonight!" Katie squealed.

"What shall we name her?" Katie asked her children, as she spooned a generous helping of rabbit and dumplings into an old cracked bowl for their new canine family member. The family had not eaten a meal that included meat in a week or so, but Katie was determined to share with the dog.

"Let's call her 'Hunter!'" her son piped up.

"Yeah, yeah!" Both young daughters agreed. "Thank you, Mama. You know we always wanted a dog of our own. That means she gets to stay here!"

From that day forward, Hunter became a loving and working member of the family

Hunter soon began walking to school each day with the children, and she waited patiently until the kids were released. She protectively saw them home and reveled in the attention they offered her. Hunter had brought change to the entire family, and it was change for the better in the midst of a difficult life.

Most afternoons when the children left the highway and crossed the desert to the old shack, Hunter headed off scouting to see what fare she might shake out of the desert scrub brush for a decent evening meal—a routine she continued for years.

Time passed, the children grew older, and eventually both girls married and left home. Then, after WWII started, Katie's son went into the Air Force to help his country. Hunter's age was showing, her muzzle had grayed, but life was easier for her now. She had only Katie to protect and she didn't need to hunt daily to keep meat on the table for only the two of them.

Sadly, the day finally came that Hunter could no longer move fast enough to catch anything. However, by then, money was being sent to my Grandma Katie from her grown children. Katie and Hunter were able to manage with their help. Favors from years long past were being returned to their mother, and the now-old dog that literally saved them during the tough times.

Katie and Hunter retired from the rigors of life in the desert, moved into town and spent their remaining years together happily. They are buried next to one another just south of town at one of the old Superior, Arizona mine cemeteries.

The stone reads: "Katie & Hunter."

Because of Max

by
Francine Baldwin-Billingslea

Yes, we all think that we have wonder dogs. But mine is—in every sense of the word.

Max has always been an in-your-face kind of dog, never pesky, but always around watching and listening, absorbing and observing, never missing out on anything. So when I was diagnosed with Stage II breast cancer, I wasn't at all surprised that Max knew something was radically wrong with me. No one that knew him was surprised at his behavior. During that time he hardly left my side. He watched my every move and often nestled next to me, cuddling and licking my bald head, letting me know he was there with me in his loving, overprotective, doggy sort of way.

One day when my daughter came by, I wrote out a list of things I needed and sent her to the store. To be perfectly honest, I didn't feel well at all and wasn't up to having company. I told her she didn't have to rush back with the items, but that she could drop them off the next day. After an hour or so of conversation and feigned laughter, I told her I was tired and needed to take a nap. She took care of a few things around the house and then left to do my shopping.

I went downstairs to get some water when suddenly everything went black. I had passed out and awoke in a pool of blood. Too weak to get up and not near the phone, all I could do was to pray for help as I went in and out of consciousness. From time to time, Max would run through the house barking, then come back and lay right beside me. At that point I knew he was my only hope. As I lay there wondering what he could do, my world became black once again.

I woke to hear the phone ringing. Unable to reach it, I lay helplessly as Max barked loudly and frantically in my face. The phone and Max both finally ceased making noise. Within a few minutes later, the phone rang again. Max barked. The third time it rang, with no other choice and praying for a miracle, I weakly whispered, "Go get it, boy. Get the phone." He simply raced around barking, for he was in his own state of panic.

When the phone stopped ringing, Max would stop barking and lay right beside me. I could feel myself growing weaker and weaker and it seemed he sensed my plight, too. Each time I drifted off, he'd lick my face and bark until I opened my eyes. It was as if he knew what must be done: keep me awake or I'd fall into an eternal sleep. The phone started again! I weakly whispered in the most commanding voice I could muster, "Go get it, boy. Get the phone."

Max ran off then returned and continued to lie beside me, licking my face. Time went by and I no longer heard the phone. When I tried to raise my head and body, in pain, weak and with absolutely no strength at all, I'd fall back into a world of hopelessness, darkness and despair.

I don't know how much time passed before I faintly remember being rushed into the hospital, my daughter leaning over me. It was several days later that I was conscious enough to understand what had occurred. I'd become extremely dehydrated, anemic and my blood pressure had dropped dangerously low, while my temperature had spiked dangerously high.

While my daughter was in the store that day, she realized she'd forgotten the list of things I needed. After calling the first time and not getting an answer, she assumed I was sleeping. The second time, she thought I was talking on the phone and didn't click over, which was a bad habit of mine. She also thought that maybe I was in the yard with Max and simply didn't hear the phone. After the third unanswered call, she became concerned.

Trying a fourth time, my daughter got a busy signal, which shouldn't have happened because I have call-waiting on my phone. She knew instantly something was wrong. Dropping everything right where she stood, she left the store and rushed back to my home. As she was putting the key in the door, she could hear Max barking frantically. When she opened the door, he jumped on her. He then used his body to push and his teeth to pull her into the kitchen, where she found me passed out on the floor. Looking around, she also noticed the phone off its cradle.

Thinking back at the series of events, Max must have instinctively sensed I was in danger. Being the obedient, intelligent dog that he is, and unbeknownst to me, he had knocked the phone off the hook after the third call. By doing so, his action not only sent out a busy signal, but a signal that I needed help. I knew he was going to do something— I just had no idea of what it would be. I prayed that whatever it was, help would arrive in time. My prayers were answered. Max was heaven-sent.

Canine in a Car

by
Carol Clouse

I decided to drive the 2,100 miles from northwest Montana to my home in southeast Pennsylvania. My Rocky Mountain cabin-building excursion was in a lull, and I missed the fall colors in the eastern Appalachians.

My sole traveling companion would be "Moccasin." A black Labrador/German Shepherd, one of Moccasin's endearing qualities was that one of her ears went up, while the other went down. She was always an integral part of any plan, and her presence invoked a certain sense of security. But in the midst of our packing preparations, I grabbed a can of Montana Grizzly Bear Pepper Spray for extra out-on-the-open-road protection—just in case.

Mapping out the journey, I decided to take the high road. Selecting the northern route, I would traverse 400 miles across northern Montana, 360 miles across northern North

Dakota, and then wander into and through Minnesota, Wisconsin and upper Michigan. At the awe-striking Mackinaw Bridge, which spanned between Lake Huron and Lake Michigan, I would turn south toward the 40-degree latitude line leading into Pennsylvania.

With an estimated total driving time of 46 hours, I divided the drive into four 12- hour days and planned ahead. I called the Lewis and Clark State Park in North Dakota, just over the Montana state line, to see if they would have a campsite available around the 20th of October.

"Yes," the park ranger said, "you should have no problem getting a site. No reservation is necessary."

My intention wasn't to camp, but rather to camp out in my car and sleep cuddled up next to my dog. I also scoped out a couple of state parks in Wisconsin as potential pit stops for my second night.

I departed from Montana early Monday morning with a heaping portion of adrenaline and enthusiasm. I was now on Route 2 heading east, but this was not a college-kid-rite-of-passage road trip. I was 51 and debatably out of my mind. OK, I wasn't out of my mind when I drove down the gravel driveway that morning, but 12 hours later, I realized I had lost some cerebral matter somewhere along the length of Route 2.

Driving across northeast Montana in October is sort of like sailing across the ocean. There aren't a whole lot of other boats. Or anything. No homes, no barns, no big red dots or Golden Arches. I was cruising at 75 mph because, incredibly, that was the speed limit on the two-lane, no-guard-rail, thin strip of a state highway. I passed an old pickup truck heading west and the old man waved at me. *He waved*, I mused to myself. Admittedly, I hadn't seen another vehicle for quite a while, and so, at a combined 150 mph, we managed to have a whiz-by, welcomed humanistic exchange. As counterpoint, drivers in my home state of Pennsylvania could be side-by-side, bumper-to-bumper, in 2 mph traffic, and it would never occur to them to have an exchange, unless you count middle finger sign language.

I had never felt quite so all alone.

The vastness was soul-searchingly scenic, but still, I was feeling like a speck of stardust in the big Montana sky. Insignificant and in solitary confinement in my car, it struck me that this this was not unlike a Native American four-day Vision Quest.

Just as the sun was settling down for the night, I arrived at the chosen state park, several miles off the main road. I followed the signs to the camping area and arrived at a nuclear holocaust. Well, that's what it felt like. *Did the world end and no one told me?* I thought. It was deserted. Empty. Eerie. Not a soul or vehicle in sight.

I drove back to the ranger's house and knocked on the door. No answer. No light green ranger truck parked anywhere. I got back in my car, and then pulled over to the curb near the main gate. I took myself and Moccasin for a pee in the grass, and then we crawled back into the car and locked the doors. And that's when I realized about the losing-my-mind thing. Fatigued, famished and a bit freaked out, I started to bawl. Before falling to sleep, I calculated and considered the option of turning around and heading back to Montana.

Before light, birdcalls had me up early and on our way. At the main road, I turned right and east. It was a classic sunny driving day. *Oh, what is this?* I wondered, thrilled that at last Route 2 had turned into a smooth, four-lane North Dakotan highway, with neatly spaced rest facilities for dogs and weary women. My cerebral mass seemed to reassemble. *Splendid.*

As I traveled eastward on the flat straight roadway into Minnesota and Wisconsin, trees accumulated and the four lanes merged back into narrow blacktop. Buildings appeared, but nothing amassed. I was still on a rural road trip. Moccasin was an awesome traveler and at the end of a successful 12-hour drive day, I pulled into a gorgeous Wisconsin state park. The park brought back the warm fuzzies of past fall camping trips in the woods of Pennsylvania. Colorfully-leaved hardwood trees, a babbling creek and no other campers—at all! Yet I felt no freaky aloneness with my car tucked in the familiar and friendly tree cover. Sleep came easy. Moccasin and I curled up for the night.

At 1 A.M., and out of nowhere, Moccasin jumped from the back seat to the front seat and began clawing away at the glass window like Edward Scissorhands, waking me out of my slumber. *What the hell?* Then I heard it. Thunder. Faint over-in-another-county thunder. My dog was inconsolable. She was a quivering psychotic mess and I knew nothing would calm her. At home, she would have gone into the shower for refuge, but nothing doing here, so I decided to just get up and drive.

I couldn't have been more than a football field from my campsite parking spot when there was a bright flash in the sky, followed by a thunder crack. Then a monsoon commenced. Wipers washed away at warp speed to no avail, and I couldn't even see the front of my car. As the downpour slightly let up, I squinted through the easing deluge and made it the two miles back to remote Route 2. Moccasin and I were in the middle of nowhere, in a blink-of-an-eye town, along a very rural highway. Yet even the smallest of towns had a bar, and, as fate would have it, there was one right at the intersection.

I had no umbrella. I couldn't leave Moccasin alone in the car for fear of her safety and my vinyl upholstery. At 1:30 A.M., I opened the old bar door and blasted in with a drenched and freaked-out dog, taut at the end of a rope, clamoring to get inside. Our entrance startled three locals and their quaint conversation, and I asked them if it was OK to bring the dog inside. They nodded. As if they had a choice.

Moccasin and I spent two hours in this Wisconsin backcountry bar. I had two rum and Cokes, but Moccasin wouldn't touch the beef treats the bartender graciously offered her. That's how much she doesn't care for thunder. When the storm stopped, I drove us back to the campsite to sleep.

Our third day brought fair weather and a much-needed walk in the woods before departure. We stopped along Lake Michigan for a brief jaunt on the beach, and then made our way across the big bridge and on down the line to a more condensed civilization. No more nice and easy Highway 2. We were on highway concrete with trucks and truck stops, which is where we crashed for our third night. I felt oddly safer in the chaos and congestion, and I knew Moccasin would alert me of any mischief.

The fourth day we drove in the rain. Because of weather and traffic, we weren't making good time. Daylight faded as I headed away from the setting sun, and the needle on the gas gauge was getting unnervingly near the letter E.

Exhausted, spent and beyond ready for a real bed, I pulled off the highway at an exit with one small gas station. At this point, I had one good credit card and no cash. I swiped my card at the pump, and it beeped "unauthorized." I tried again and it beeped again. I went inside and the cashier girl gave it a swipe. Nope. It wouldn't go through.

"But," I told her, "I know there's credit on it. I've been using it for the past four days on my drive from Montana." I was beside myself and that part of me must have looked awfully defeated, because the cashier girl took pity.

"Oh," she offered, "sometimes if you use your card in too many different places, they think it's stolen and put a hold on it."

What? I called the credit card company and had to give blood to prove I was myself—an out-of-mind lady driving across the country with her dog—and they allowed the purchase. I went back to the pump to try again. Thankfully, it worked.

As I began quenching my tank, a man casually walked over to me and asked, "Is that your dog over there?" *OMG!* In my frenzied frustration, I had left the car door open and Moccasin was taking her black-girl self for a dark evening stroll, which was a dangerous situation because she was hard to see.

I called to her and Moccasin looked at me, as confused as I felt. She then came and reluctantly got back into the car again. *She must think this is where we're going to live for the rest of our lives—inside a Honda Fit.* We arrived in Pennsylvania before midnight, and once home, we melted into our beds like amoebas, safe and sound.

A few days later, I was driving on the highway, with Moccasin in the back seat. I had just slowed to exit at a ramp when I heard a sudden noise behind me. The noise imitated the sound of air releasing from a balloon or whipped cream coming out of a can. But louder. I instinctively turned to see what was happening when orange mist spewed into my face. My mind raced and searched for comprehension as a voice inside said *Why in hell is there orange spray paint in my car!?*

My autopilot motor skills had appropriately taken to slowing down the car and pulling it off onto the road's shoulder. As soon as the car stopped, I made my rapid escape while coming to the acute realization that I had been hit in the face with the Grizzly Bear Pepper Spray, which I had forgotten all about. Somehow, someway, all the stars lined up and Jupiter danced her thing, which, in turn, caused Moccasin to trip off the spray's safety release, step down on the trigger and hit me in the face with a blast of pepper spray. And not any pepper spray, mind you, but spray potent enough to thwart a grizzly bear attack!

I could not breathe. At all. My throat was completely closed. I could not breathe and although aware of the sheer futility, I dialed 911. There was no doubt in my mind that I would be dead before an ambulance ever got to me, and I considered this an absolutely absurd way to go.

The 911 operator answered the call and asked, "911—what's your emergency?" I said nothing. Silence. I couldn't breathe and I couldn't talk.

Slowly, muffled sounds of great effort began to emerge

from my throat and the 911 operator said, "It sounds like you need an ambulance. Can you tell me where you are?"

Well, no. I can't talk, and even if I could, I don't know how to tell you where I am. I flagged down the next vehicle and the woman in the passenger seat didn't just flip me off, thinking I was an escaped mental patient. By now, I was breathing a little better, but still could barely talk. I handed her my phone and motioned for her to talk to the 911 operator. I was then able to tell her that I got hit with Grizzly Bear Pepper Spray . . . by my dog, no less!

I then returned to my car and checked on Moccasin. She seemed fine. Thankfully, the pepper spray didn't make direct contact with her, even though some small amounts of residual spray were sure to have landed on her.

By the time the ambulance arrived, I was breathing better, but my eyes and face were on fire. The EMT then immediately went to my car and began to roll down the windows—all the way—saying the dog needed air. I immediately put the windows back up, explaining that my Montana dog would jump out of the window and into highway traffic, becoming the city equivalent of a road-kill deer. Wolves she's familiar with. Highway traffic, not so much. We compromised by my getting Moccasin on a leash and out of the car.

After confirming we were both OK, the EMT suggested I go somewhere to thoroughly rinse off. My house was relatively close by, so Moccasin and I got our first ride in an ambulance. I rinsed us both and got a ride back to retrieve my car.

I wondered if anyone ever died from getting sprayed with Grizzly Bear Pepper Spray. But then, why would anyone *ever* get sprayed with Grizzly Bear Pepper Spray?

By this time, the out-of-my-mind feeling had subsided and was replaced by a new layer of self-confidence. There's nothing like traveling solo to test your endurance—mentally, emotionally, physically and socially. I mention socially because it's said that traveling is a true test of friendship. And when you travel alone, you really learn to love your companion, even the canine variety, as well as the best friend that lies inside yourself.

CHAPTER
FOUR

Unleashed!

And you'd best watch out!

Thalia

by
Betty Guenette

I convinced my husband we needed a dog.

"Not one of those little yappy ones," he said, frowning.

"No, dear. No little noisy ones."

"And not one of those shedding, rat types either. They leave messy hair all over the furniture and clothes. And they make me sneeze," he added.

"Yes, dear. I'll find a large breed, non-allergic and intelligent."

"Well, OK, I guess. At least we can walk it for exercise."

OK, so no furry cuddly dogs, I thought. But I was thrilled he had agreed!

After careful study, I chose an apricot-colored Standard Poodle. My dreams of dog ownership should have been great. However, I jinxed myself by calling her "Thalia"—a name denoting the Greek Goddess of Comedy.

We breezed through two back-to-back sessions of training classes. Thalia passed both, but missed our expectations of obeying the rules at home. Her hyperactive nature just accelerated with age. She leapt and jumped through the air with joy and greeted our visitors by trying to knock them down to her level, dribbling on the floor in her exuberance. Timeout in the cage met with noisy resistance. Emitting high-pitched crescendos of howling intensity, she demanded release from such unthinkable imprisonment. I'm certain her howling meant, "How could you do this to me?"

Thalia was a habitual toilet drinker. Since we couldn't get her to change, I trained my husband to put both toilet lids down. One night, I got up, half-asleep with a full bladder and plopped down on the cold, closed toilet seat. Not fun.

Next, we tried installing baby gates to bar Thalia from selected rooms like the bathroom. When I saw her sail straight over the gate from a standing position, we switched to closing doors.

When my sisters visited, Thalia displayed my ineptitude with dog training by going into her frenzy mode. She bounced through the living room, barely touching down as she flew from couch to couch, greeting our new company with slobbers, dribbles and barks. When I waved goodbye to my visitors at the door, I heard Thalia slurping away in the bathroom. All that activity made her thirsty and my guests didn't shut the bathroom door. *Sure hope they flushed,* I secretly mused.

Thalia loved underwear. Laundry days became tug-of-wars with many torn results. On non-laundry days, she would fish the undies out of the hamper and drop them like gifts at anyone's feet. These presents often greeted visitors after she peed near or even, occasionally, on them. During enthusiastic episodes of hers, I became the daily mop woman.

One morning my husband, sporting a wicked grin, asked me if he'd gotten lucky during the night and just couldn't remember.

"Huh?" I asked, startled.

He held up a pair of my panties that he had found rolled up in the sheets as he got out of bed.

I shook my head. "That darn dog again."

"Well, you know she shouldn't be on our bed."

"Yes, dear. I'll try to remember to shut our door."

I shook my head again and left the bedroom. I thought better about not telling him that yesterday I had caught Thalia lying on his side of the bed, chewing up the bristled toilet bowl brush. Yes, our Greek God of Comedy had had the last laugh!

Thalia and Betty

Stop, Thief!

by

Gina Mulligan

When we brought home a yellow Labrador Retriever puppy, we knew he had big paws to fill. A month earlier, we had lost our 14-year-old Labrador and thought a puppy would ease our grief.

We named our new pup "Coda." Now, you're probably thinking this is going to be a *Marley and Me* story, but it isn't. For the most part, Coda's a good dog. But, in all seriousness, our little bundle of joy's a thief.

I'm convinced that if Coda had thumbs, by now he'd be behind bars in an orange jumpsuit, trading favors for cigarettes. Like most offenders, his life of crime started at a young age, with misdemeanors such as lifting socks from the hamper. And I've lost count of how many toys he's nabbed out of unsuspecting hands. His favorite grabs are those plastic Chuckits used to throw tennis balls, not to mention the balls themselves. He's also liberated two cell phones and a set of car keys.

If I hadn't stopped him, he'd probably be in Mexico by now.

As Coda grew, so did his reputation. At our local dog park, he's known as "Crafty Coda" for stealing leashes and dumping over a very large water tub, and then dragging it around the park. But, by far, Coda's best steal was a shoe. This isn't such a big deal, since most dogs do steal shoes. But Coda, you see, has definitely earned his nickname.

If there's one thing Coda has, its flair. Picture a friendly dog park on a mild sunny day. It isn't crowded, but there's a nice gathering. Dogs are romping while owners sit at benches in the shade or gather in small groups to chat. Even Coda seems content, bounding after a chocolate-colored Boxer.

All is affable, and I look away for just a moment. When I look back, Coda has abandoned his friend and trots over to a lady on a bench. His mark is sitting crossed legged and wearing a new pair of leather flip-flops. Coda charms her with his best wiggling and wagging as he approaches. He seems genuinely enthusiastic, so I don't intervene. The woman smiles and reaches out to pet Coda's head, but instead of waiting for his pat, Coda yanks a flip-flop right off the woman's foot and makes a dash for it.

Everyone, except the lady now missing a shoe, chases Coda around the park. I worry his slobber is ruining the shoe leather. But why worry about slobber when there's a mud puddle in the corner? Yep, Coda gave up the chase and dropped the shoe right in the mud. I apologize to the woman, and offer to turn my boy over to the authorities. The now one-shoed woman asks that I rinse her muddy sandal with the hose—which I did, of course— then she limps off with her Boxer. To this day, I still wonder if the shoe survived, but I'll never know because I never saw the woman again. Who can blame her? The dog park is obviously a dangerous area, riddled with hoodlums.

Since the incident, I have walked Coda on a leash and stayed away from the park. This seems like the best way to protect the neighborhood. Sometimes my husband and I cringe when we think back to the day we brought Coda home. Then we remind ourselves that Coda is a loveable dog with many fine and loyal canine qualities. Still, having a felon in the family comes with responsibility.

On a walk just the other day, we passed a garage sale. The new neighbors hadn't been warned about the local menace, and they placed open boxes with children's books and stuffed animals close to the sidewalk. Too close. Crafty Coda made his move. You can imagine what happened next.

Sunny Day

by
Rolland Love

During the winter of 1948, my best pal Sunny, an Australian Shepherd pup, went hunting with me on a bitter-cold day. I was 9 years old.

While we walked through the countryside, and without any warning whatsoever, Sunny jumped a rabbit and disappeared over the hill. I called and called for him with no luck. After about 30 minutes, I got so scared I began to cry. He had never done anything like that before. He was still so young that I was terrified he might get lost.

I started to run toward the house to tell Dad what had happened. Then I heard the sound of Sunny's deep, gruff bark. I turned around and saw that he was dragging something toward me as he wagged his tail. When he got closer, I could see that the black-and-white object was a dead skunk. It took some serious scrubbing by my very unhappy Mom to get rid of that smell. I was afraid she was going to scrub the skin right off that poor dog!

To this day, I remember Sunny's antics like it was yesterday. He was a beautiful and intelligent animal, very fast and could jump so high I had to build a taller fence around the backyard. Without it, I can only imagine what kind of mischief he'd have found or created, but I knew it was bound to be crazy!

One summer afternoon, I sat on the bank of the farm's pond, daydreaming and listening to a red-winged blackbird sing. Sunny was milling about doing what dogs do, sniffing, looking for squirrels and coming to me now and then for a pat on his head.

Dad was nearby fixing the corncrib door the wind had torn off, while at the same time trying to keep an eye on me and Sunny. Suddenly and like a shot, Sunny plunged into the water right in front of me. Barking and biting at the sparkling droplets that splashed in front of his face, he swam toward a flock of Canada geese, herding them along as they honked and flapped their wings.

About 20 feet from the bank, the geese seemed to realize they had Sunny outnumbered. They did an about-face, honking loudly with their necks outstretched, and swam after Sunny. He headed back toward me with a wide-eyed look of panic. He churned the water frantically with his front legs.

By that time, the commotion had caught Dad's attention. "You better help Sunny!" he yelled. "Geese are mean as the devil. They can drown a dog."

A couple of the geese pecked at Sunny's skinny black tail. The rest honked and flapped their wings. I picked up a rock and threw it at the flock, then waded into the water, yelling at the birds. Sunny swam past me as if he was spooked by the devil—just like Dad said! Finally, the geese finally backed off when they realized I wasn't going to allow them in the area. Yelping like the pup he was, Sunny splashed out onto the bank, and without taking time to shake off the water, he high-tailed it for the house.

Dad and I laughed so hard we could hardly stand up.

"What's goin' on out there?" Mom yelled, walking out the back door.

I ran to the house and told Mom what happened. She got so tickled that she had to sit down before she toppled right off the steps. The geese were still honking in the background as Sunny walked up to me. I patted his head. He wagged his tail, licked my hand and finally shook the water off his coat.

Sunny lived to be 15 years old and went with us everywhere, even on many a coon hunt. Nothing seemed to spook him. However, never again did he make the mistake of diving into the pond to swim after a flock of geese.

The Legendary Miss Ellie

by
Maggie Ryland, DVM

On the early May morning she encountered the cougar, Miss Ellie weighed 80 pounds. I know this as fact; she had been weighed the day before when getting her first booster vaccinations. My vet had remarked that she would probably add a few more pounds before she reached her adult weight in a couple of months.

Still a puppy, I thought to myself as we headed off into the woods along a logging road that formed a spur at the north end of the lake.

I had moved from Seattle to this isolated area in northeastern Washington state a year and a half earlier. I left behind traffic congestion, crime and the high stress of urban living for the beauty and quiet of a subalpine forest surrounding a small pristine lake. Miss Ellie had been one of my earliest acquisitions, a friend to help ease my adjustment to a more solitary and close-to-nature lifestyle, a companion with whom I could hike and explore this new and unfamiliar environment.

I had named her after the matriarch of the Ewing clan in the *Dallas* television series because, like Barbara Bel Geddes' character, she was blond, buxom and bossy. Even as a 7-week-old puppy, small enough to spend the first night in her new home sleeping under the TV stand, she was a yellow Labrador Retriever with a strong will and mind of her own.

So when she trotted off ahead of me, I didn't have a second thought. The ground was still covered in several inches of coarse granular snow where the early spring sun had been unable to penetrate. Thick pines and Douglas fir grew on either side of the trail and I was walking more slowly than Miss Ellie preferred. *I'll catch up with her shortly*, I thought, as she rounded an uphill bend 30 yards in front of me and disappeared.

I continued up the steep trail, walking carefully to avoid the deepest patches of snow, when I suddenly heard loud excited barking. Still unconcerned, I assumed that Miss Ellie had come upon a white-tailed deer or a grouse, perhaps even a flock of wild turkeys, and was expressing her frustration at their hasty departures. These escapades had happened before. They were no big deal, all a part of our shared nature experience. I hiked on, confident that I would soon catch up and be able to identify the cause of her excitement.

As I approached the bend in the trail, the barking stopped and everything suddenly became silent. Birdsong ceased, and the subtle rustling of aspen leaves and the *tchrring* of the omnipresent red squirrels subsided. All at once I heard a furious thrashing of snow and saw Miss Ellie churning back down the trail toward me. Her legs moved so fast that they became a blur in the icy cloud of white crystals being thrown into the air by her flailing paws.

She hurtled down the snowy slope toward me, and as I focused my gaze behind her, I saw an enormous cinnamon-colored animal with a tail as long as a picnic table. The animal was nearly three times Ellie's size and was cantering closely behind her, close enough that if it had fully extended its front legs, it would easily have touched her. I thought of images from countless *National Geographic* episodes I'd seen on TV, images of lions and cheetahs bringing down hapless wildebeests and exhausted gazelles.

But this huge animal behind Miss Ellie was moving effortlessly, its long spine arching and extending with every relaxed, elongated stride. With its unhurried gait, it looked more like a thoroughbred running a cool-down lap at the end of a race than a predator in pursuit of prey.

A deer? I stupidly asked myself. *No, deer don't have tails,* I reminded myself in the same instant, as my mind tried to make sense of what my incredulous eyes were seeing. "What the … ? Oh, S_ _t! Oh, S_ _! Oh S_ _t, s_ _t, s_ _t!!! It's a COUGAR!!!"

Miss Ellie continued to race toward me, legs flailing, snow flying and then she disappeared behind my back, out of sight. As she vanished behind me, the cougar noticed my presence for the first time. It slowed awkwardly to a trot, and then to a stop. Now it was standing motionless, about 20 feet squarely in front of me on the narrow dirt road. We were surrounded by deep forest. The world was silent. We were face to face with each other and neither of us seemed to know what to do. Miss Ellie was nowhere to be seen.

The next seconds seemed to unfold in slow motion, and all the while I had the sense that I was observing the scene from a distance, not a participant as much as a witness. Somehow I managed to resurrect the knowledge gleaned from my newly purchased books on native flora and fauna. I was supposed to make myself look big. I was supposed to sound fierce. Under no circumstance was I to turn my back and run. I was supposed to establish eye contact. I was supposed to assume a dominant presence.

"Crap," I murmured as I fumbled for the zipper on my windbreaker, awkwardly opening the jacket and pulling each half of it away from my body and out to the side, making flaps like those of a flying squirrel. I began to shout and flap my jacket with my arms, trying to be as big, bold, loud and intimidating as I could be. I remember thinking I was likely going to wake the neighbors and then remembered that there were no neighbors for more than a mile. "S_ _t," I repeated. "S_ _t, s_ _t, s_ _t!" Then louder, "AAAAAAHHHHHH!!! SCRAAAAAAAM!!! GOAAWAAAAYYY!!!!"

I flapped, I screamed, and I kept on screaming. I shrieked and cursed and yelled until my throat hurt and I heard myself becoming hoarse.

I stared into the amber eyes of that magnificent beast and let it know that I would stand my ground and what was it doing chasing my dog anyway. It needed to be gone, out of my sight, I mean GONE, right then and there. It had no business scaring us and it needed to VAMOOOOOOOOOSE!!! It just stared right back at me.

I remember thinking that its head was unusually small for

such a large body, that its black and white facial markings were exquisite in contrast to the rest of its cinnamon-colored coat, and I recall noticing that it had tufts of fur hanging loosely from under its neck, as if it needed a good brushing to fully remove its winter undercoat. Still, I continued to flap and scream until I thought I couldn't shriek any more.

Finally, after what seemed like an eternity of shouting, jacket flapping and staring, the cougar swiveled one ear to the side, then back again. Then it made the same motion with the other ear, as if trying to identify the source of a distant, slightly distracting sound. It was a subtle gesture to be sure, but one that I immediately recognized, having spent my life around pet cats that I adored. It was a gesture that communicated a sense of ease, of mild curiosity perhaps, but an indication that there was no overriding sense of alarm. Interest, yes, but nothing to get a cat's adrenaline flowing. A defusing body sign, the language of capitulation to circumstance, nothing more. I stopped shouting and put my arms down. My frantic bluffing had apparently worked.

The puzzled cat looked slowly to its left, then to its right, and then looked back at me. For a final time I met its gaze. Then the cougar turned and loped off the trail through the tall trees back into the woods, its amber body and its long ropelike tail disappearing into the forest.

At this point Miss Ellie, who evidently had been safely viewing the scene somewhere behind my back, reemerged into my field of vision. I watched aghast as she took off into the woods after the cougar, barking furiously once more. I stood motionless, not knowing if I should call her back and risk having the cougar follow her again or leave her to her own devices. *Calling her back to me is futile*, I reminded myself. *She never comes when she's called anyway.*

As I waited in stunned silence on the trail, unable to think clearly or even to move with purpose, Miss Ellie reappeared from between the trees a dozen feet to my right. She was panting but obviously unhurt, and she seemed somehow triumphant, as if she had indeed chased away that ferocious beast. The beast which, without her timely and courageous intervention, would likely have made dinner out of both of us. It was almost as if Miss Ellie Ewing herself was there, standing in front of Southfork Ranch holding a smoking shotgun and saying with satisfaction, "This is how we deal with trespassers."

Over the next several days my voice returned and I was able to recount our adventure to my neighbors, most of whom had lived in the area for decades but had never seen a cougar face-to-face. I described how this enormous cougar could easily have weighed as much as 240 pounds, as it was clearly three times Miss Ellie's size. After all, I had seen them nose to tail and could attest to their relative length and bulk.

The story must have spread beyond to a broader, more populous audience. Nearly two years later, Miss Ellie and I were stopped by a couple in a white pickup truck as we were walking along the gravel road that runs along the eastern side of the lake. By then, Miss Ellie was nearly 3 years old, weighed 90 pounds and was as bossy as ever. The unfamiliar pair rolled down a window and asked, "Is that the cougar dog? Is that the one that scared away the really, really big cougar?"

I looked down at Miss Ellie, her fur the color of corn silk.

I stroked her broad head and touched the softness of her ears with my fingers. "This dog?" Then I stopped, looking down once again at my best friend and outdoor companion. I reconsidered.

"Yup, this is the one. Without her, I'd likely have been a cougar's lunch."

Miss Ellie looked up at me as if to express impatience. Her expression said to get going again, to pick up the pace, to hit the road girlfriend, to move it out and be on our way. Hustle your bustle. I've got places to go, moose tracks to follow, things to smell, woods to patrol. Come on, sister, time's a wasting.

But she never denied a thing. Apparently, like everyone else in this neck of the woods, she loves a good story.

Maggie and Miss Ellie

The Runt

by
Ireta Black

Back in the early 1970s, my teenage daughter Theresa was being courted by a boy who was two years older than her. Ken was a nice guy and my husband, Gene, and I thought well of him.

Theresa's 15th birthday was coming up, and Ken had no money to buy her a present. Wanting to get Theresa something special, Ken brought her a puppy he got for free from some relatives.

We learned that the puppy was the runt of the litter. Theresa was thrilled and named her "Trudy." The dog was a black and white Terrier and very, very small, even when she grew into an adult, topping the scales at 9 pounds.

A year later, Trudy became a mom, birthing three pups. We never quite figured out who the daddy was, but he had to have been a larger dog because the puppies eventually outgrew their mom. Even though Trudy was once again the runt, she kept her kids in line. For example, I had hung Gene's blue jeans on the line to dry one day, to the puppies' delight. They ran and jumped and grabbed for the dangling jeans, having great fun. But momma dog didn't approve of their game, and told them so by running and jumping head-on into them, knocking each one to the ground. Startled, they listened to their mom and never did that ever again!

When Theresa graduated from high school, she and Ken married and got a place of their own. Trudy and her three kids stayed with us on our fenced-in acre of land, which included fruit and nut trees and a large garden. And Trudy was eventually spayed, because four dogs were enough for us!

Trudy was a very intelligent and helpful dog. Gene and I spent much time in our garden, and Trudy was always with us, watching what we were doing. She was especially interested when we went tomato-worm hunting. Those dang worms would eat our tomatoes, and we didn't like that! We would search for a worm, pull it off, and then squish it with our foot. Those worms were yucky and green and very hard to find.

One evening when we were in the garden, we saw little Trudy in the tomato plants. I was just about ready to holler at her to get out of the tomato patch when suddenly I realized she had a big tomato worm in her mouth. She carried the worm to the edge of the patch, dropped it, and then pawed it into the ground. She was doing exactly what Gene and I did when we caught worms! After that, Trudy was allowed into the tomato patch to hunt for worms, and she received lots of praise from us for her help.

Gene's parents lived nearby, and were robbed one night while they were asleep. Concerned that this would happen again, we decided Trudy should live with them. This worked out well for everyone, especially Trudy, who was ready for retirement from her days of puppy-wrangling and tomato-worm hunting. Trudy had such a sharp bark that she would alert my in-laws of any intruders or visitors. When Trudy was with us for those many years, we spoiled her here and there. When she moved in with my elderly in-laws, they spoiled her rotten and Trudy lived her final days as a special companion and beloved lap dog.

Even though Trudy was small in size, being the runt of the litter didn't mean one thing to her or to us. Trudy was bigger than life and everyone knew it. Size doesn't matter—it's what's inside, and Trudy was all heart.

Rocky Loses by a TKO

by
Becky Povich

I wasn't with Ron the day he spotted the "Free Puppies" sign. Later he claimed when he almost passed it, our car spontaneously, and very much on its own, swerved into the gravel driveway and lurched to a stop, flinging grit and tiny pebbles in all directions. Our magic automobile reacted the same way whenever it neared "Garage Sale" and "Yard Sale" signs, too.

"You should've seen them, honey," Ron grinned as he recounted the story to me. "Those puppies kept climbing and tumbling out of their cardboard box. Each one scampering around the lawn was cuter than the next. Little fuzzy bundles of black and brown rolling around . . . ."

"Oh, I would've loved to have seen that," I interrupted.

Ron nodded and continued, "When I crouched down and called to the pups, one, in particular, ran all the way across the yard and practically jumped into my arms. That did it. I told the owner I'd be happy to take that little guy off his hands and give him a good home."

I was thrilled with his decision. The puppy was small, newly weaned, cute and cuddly. His soft fur was mostly black, with tiny patches of light brown above each eye and on all four legs. We weren't sure of the puppy's breed, but it didn't matter at that moment. My then 11-year-old son, Scott, named our new pup. He chose "Rocky" and it seemed to fit perfectly the moment he bestowed it upon our newest member of the family.

Over the next few months, Rocky grew bigger by the day, the hour, the minute. At six months old, his paws were almost as big as the palm of my hand. That's when we learned Rocky was part Gordon Setter and part some-kind-of-a-really-big-dog.

You know how intelligent adults sometimes do the stupidest things? At the time, we lived in a small two-bedroom apartment on the second floor of an old complex. Ron and I both worked full-time and Scott, obviously, went to school. Still, we thought leaving Rocky home alone all those hours during the day was perfectly OK. After all, he was paper-trained. But we soon learned he was not house-trained.

Our beloved puppy became bored, so he searched for things in the apartment to amuse himself. Rocky's antics became so commonplace that I knew every weekday—at 3:15, when Scott got home from school—my office phone would ring, and Scott would recite Rocky's activities for the day. I didn't even say "Hello" anymore. This daily phone call became the highlight of the afternoon for my co-workers.

"What did he do today?" I'd sigh to Scott. The men and women in my office would stop what they were doing. A hush of silence filled the room as they leaned my way and sat perfectly still.

As I listened to Scott's account, my facial expressions would change from shock or surprise to disbelief or anger. On some days I just gasped and snorted a word or two:

"He did what?"

"Oh, my gosh!"

"Are you kidding me?"

"Can you clean it up?"

"Did you tell him 'bad dog'?"

"Well, close the cabinets."

"Well, close your closet."

"Well, shut the drawers."

I'd then hang up and fill in the details for my eager colleagues.

Rocky's days were always filled with mischief. He had a fondness for standard dog provisions—shoes, newspapers, magazines, tennis balls—pretty much anything he could find in the apartment. He even teethed on my lovely Bentwood rocker. I wondered and worried how he could eat the things he did and not get sick. He chewed up and evidently swallowed chunks of our dilapidated couch, including foam stuffing, fabric and wood. And one day he managed to dig out our wedding album and chomp on some of the photos, leaving visible bite marks.

In a way, I was surprised our downstairs neighbors never

complained of noise, but I assumed they worked during the day, too. Then one morning I received the dreaded phone call. It was from my elderly apartment manager.

"Hello, Becky?" I immediately recognized her raspy smoker's voice.

"Mildred! What's wrong?"

"I think you better come home. There's been a lot of racket going on in your apartment, and some people have complained." She coughed and hacked for a while before continuing, "I walked over that way and heard it before I got to your building. Your dog was barking like crazy and it sounded like things were falling and breaking inside."

"Oh, my gosh. I'll get there as soon as I can."

I slammed the phone down, grabbed my purse and dashed out of the office. "I gotta go. Rocky's in trouble," I hollered to my co-workers.

I barely remember driving home or pulling into the apartment building's parking lot. I was too preoccupied with images floating around in my mind. *What could possibly have happened?* I thought to myself. I ran into our building and dashed up the flight of stairs. It was absolutely quiet when I reached our door, which I hadn't expected. I hesitated, and then silently slid my key into the lock and slowly turned it, afraid of what I would see.

As I swung open the door, I immediately saw Rocky sprawled on the floor, apparently exhausted from the morning's events. Scattered all around him were pieces of my once-beautiful massive philodendron, missing so many leaves it resembled a vine. Most of the tiny nails, which served as a trellis in the wall, also were gone. *I hope he didn't eat them, too*, I worried.

I quietly stepped inside the apartment and surveyed the damage. Tiptoeing between little mounds of dirt, stems and leaves, I knew my cherished plant would never be the same again. The situation was so terrible that it was actually funny, and I couldn't help laughing. That's when Rocky looked up at me with his tired, sad eyes. He didn't even lift his head.

I'm sure he's humiliated. I bent down and patted him. I then whispered soothing words. "Poor baby, Rocky. What happened here today? Did that bad old plant attack you?"

I smiled and he began to wag his tail, slapping it against the hardwood floor. That's when he stood up and I noticed that dirt was also in his fur. It was in his ears. It was in his nostrils. He began to shake from head to tail and dirt flew in every direction. As he walked over to his water bowl, I bent down to dig through the layers of soil and found some nails. I was fairly certain he hadn't actually swallowed any, but if he had, it wasn't many and I was sure he'd be OK. We always said he had the stomach of a goat—nothing made that dog sick.

I should've expected something like this to happen. Often when Rocky loped past that plant, the sheer movement caused the leaves to flutter and wave. He seemed a bit skittish and occasionally growled at it.

It was only a matter of time until the two would battle. Pound for pound, that big lug outweighed his opponent by 50 pounds. But the philodendron had the secret element—the element of surprise. Poor Rocky never knew what hit him. I'd say he lost by a TKO, and there was plenty of evidence to prove it.

Scott, Rocky and Becky

Payday

by
Nelson O. Ottenhausen

As a captain in the United States Army during early April of 1970, I was assigned to the post commander's staff at Fort McCoy, Wisconsin, as assistant operations officer. My duties consisted of supervising the in-processing and out-processing of Army IRRs (Individual Ready Reservists) throughout the early spring, summer and early fall. Also, I was charged to fill personnel vacancies in U.S. Army Reserve and National Guard units while they conducted their two-week annual field training at Fort McCoy. The replacements were mostly U.S. Army enlisted men, with an occasional company grade officer, ordered to military active duty for a two-week period to fulfill a reserve obligation as part of their five- or seven-year enlistment program. We also processed a small number of reserve career officers who volunteered for a two-week assignment to qualify the year for retirement points.

My staff at the time consisted of one young second lieutenant, fresh out of Officers Candidate School at Fort Sill, Oklahoma, five NCOs (Non Commissioned Officers) of various grades from a master sergeant to corporal, three privates (one was my personal driver) and one civilian, a female secretary. Each enlisted man was a specialist in their MOS (Military Occupational Specialty) for administration, travel or finance. Administration consisted of one staff sergeant and a private first class clerk, processing required forms for various administrative reasons. The travel section had one sergeant who issued vouchers for commercial travel and helped those who traveled by POV (Privately Own Vehicle) to apply for reimbursement of travel expenses. In the finance section, there were three payroll specialists, a staff sergeant, a corporal and a private first class.

About midway through the summer, the second lieutenant took an approved three-day leave and came back to post with a year-old, full-grown Saint Bernard dog, about the size of a Shetland pony. The dog seemed well behaved and gentle enough, so when the lieutenant asked if he could keep it in his office, I said yes. However, within an hour, I realized I had made a terrible mistake—this animal was not an indoor pet. He roamed throughout the office, disturbed personnel and slobbered on everything.

Since the lieutenant couldn't keep the dog in the Bachelor Officer's Quarters, I told him if he wanted to keep the dog on post, he had to chain his pet to the outside of the office building. There the dog stayed for the rest of the summer, constantly annoying me. He banged on my office floor when he moved around because of his enormous size and lack of ground clearance to the floor of the old WWII single-floor, headquarters-type office building. After a few weeks, I began to tolerate the racket and the dog stayed on.

During that year's cycle and near the end of summer, we only processed one field grade officer—a lieutenant colonel—and as God would have it, somebody screwed up his payroll. So, on the morning of his out-processing day, he came stomping into the building and yelled, "Who the hell's in charge here?!"

The secretary scurried into my office and said, "There's an irate man in the outer office."

"Yes, I heard," I said.

I decided to ask the colonel into my office to discuss the matter away from other office personnel, but he caught me at the doorway and told me in no uncertain terms that he was unhappy because his paycheck was not at the finance office. He had a long drive ahead of him and wanted to get underway as soon as possible. By his comments, I could tell he did not have the utmost confidence in my finance personnel, stating a position of their heads being somewhere in the lower part of their anatomy. Several times he made reference to their family lineage and declared their intelligence level as being nonexistent, but not using those terms.

After a few minutes of tolerating his rants, I managed to calm him down and then turned to the master sergeant standing a few feet away. "Sergeant, please see that the colonel is paid as soon as possible so he can be on his way."

"Yes, sir!" The master sergeant then turned to the finance staff sergeant at the desk behind him and with a stern tone in his voice, he ordered, "Get on the colonel's problem, and see to it that he's paid ASAP."

After pausing a second to find the right payroll record and to collect his thoughts, the finance sergeant turned to the finance corporal at the desk behind him, handed him a folder and growled, "Corporal, get your ass in gear and get the colonel paid!"

Getting up from his desk with the folder in hand, the corporal hurried across the room to the payroll clerk's desk, threw down the folder and yelled, "OK, Private Dumb Ass, here's the colonel's records. You screwed this up—you fix it!"

The corporal then spewed out what seemed like a five-minute torrent of abusive language at the private. When the corporal finished his chewing-out, the berated private rose from his desk, and without a word, headed for the door.

The colonel looked at me with a shocked and puzzled look on his face, and then turned and shouted to the private, "Where the hell you going?"

The private continued walking as he replied, "Sir, outside to kick the dog."

There's a Pit Bull in My House

by

Joanne Faries

Five years after his high school graduation, my stepson Kevin completed his Marine Corps duties and was honorably discharged as a sergeant. Upon entering the armed forces, he left our home as a boy. But now he was returning home to Texas as a man and a husband.

Having married a couple of years earlier Kevin and his wife Maria had a baby of sorts—a Pit Bull puppy named "Rusty." Kevin remembered what I had always said over the years when he was younger, "You may have as many animals as you want, once you have your own place." He honored my advice and waited until he was on his own to get a dog.

Kevin is his father's son. No little pipsqueak dogs for those two. Instead, Kevin went full-steam ahead and picked out the scariest dog on the planet—my worst nightmare—although a Doberman or Rottweiler are close seconds.

A month prior to their big move home, there were lots

of phone calls between Kevin and his father, who is my husband, Ray. Kevin researched apartments online and asked Ray to check some out in person, on his behalf. Mailed documents and faxes flew between Texas and their then-current home in San Diego. Kevin learned a lot in the Marines, including strategic planning and execution of said plans. He had money coordinated, a targeted move-in date, a U-Haul truck and a job interview ready in the wings.

Over Memorial Weekend, 2005, Kevin called Ray. "I'm officially signed out of the Marines. Maria and I are heading east!" With the truck crammed with furniture, a puppy on board, and Kevin driving like a maniac, they made good time and were ahead of schedule. A total surprise, Kevin called, informing us they would be in town a day earlier than expected. Matter of fact, he said, "We're in Fort Worth. Be there in 20 minutes."

It was a Saturday afternoon and we had expected them on Sunday, their official moving day! Ray ran to the grocery store for ingredients to make his famous sour cream chicken enchiladas. I got out of the pool where I was relaxing and enjoying the day and cleaned up quick. I also made sure the guest room was presentable; in an insane lapse of judgment on my part, during that surprise call, I told Kevin they could spend Saturday night at our house. As I plumped pillows, I questioned myself. *Why am I allowing a Pit Bull in my house?*

Screech! Truck brakes announced their arrival and we walked out to greet our tired troopers. Both kids said, "Man, it's hot here."

After welcoming them and congratulating Kevin, Ray gave them grief for being California woosies. "If you can't take the heat . . . ."

"Yeah, yeah. We're not used to running an air conditioner."

Kevin had an armful of wiggling muscular puppy while he talked, and then officially introduced us to our fur grandbaby. Rusty had a white-gray body with bullseye markings. Kevin put him down on the ground and Rusty sniffed, barked, jumped, scampered and peed. Fearless, he ran circles in the field next to our home and pooped with abandon. He was bigger than I expected, with way more energy, too. Plus, he had that Pit Bull face—those teeth, that jowl and the power to tear someone from limb to limb. Suddenly, I found myself re-thinking my generosity as I watched Rusty gnaw on our tiny crepe myrtle tree. *At least it's not one of our leg bones.*

"Well, you're back in Texas, Kevin, and far from an ocean breeze," I said, adding my two cent's worth to the weather small talk. "Are you hungry? Your dad has enchiladas in the oven, and your brother Chris should be here soon."

"That sounds wonderful." Kevin swayed a bit. He was excited to be home, but weary.

"Now, Joanne, is it OK for us to stay?" Maria kindly asked. "We have a cage for Rusty and he sleeps through the night."

This was my one chance to renege. I paused and the sound of Rusty's teeth chomping on his stick echoed in my head. His puppy eyes had a gleam of potential evil, not that they glowed red, but they could. To break the awkward silence, I lied. "Yes. I told Ray to say it would be fine. It's just one night. If it were a week, I might have issues."

"He'll be good," Kevin promised.

Rusty leaped around Kevin, asking to play. "Won't you be

a good boy? Yeah, that's my boy," Kevin said to Rusty, as the dog clamped down on a stick and held on while Kevin swung him around.

He's a puppy, a mere puppy, I thought, nervous and on edge. I excused myself and went inside to set the table for dinner. But before I did, I said, "Kevin, I do have to ask that the dog stay out back while we eat. I can't have him underfoot during dinner."

"Oh, OK. But I was going to feed him at the table. He could sit on my lap," Kevin said, jokingly.

At the dinner table, we dug in to our Tex-Mex feast and caught up on all of the news. We talked over each other, asked questions, joked and enjoyed dinner together. Chris got up to mix more margaritas. Maria rose for a refill and then paused.

"I think I saw something out front," she said, with a puzzled look on her face.

"We've had some big squirrels scampering about," I mentioned, dismissing her concern.

"No, it's Rusty."

Maria ran for the front door. Kevin dropped his fork and followed. Ray stood and drew the lacy drapes back for a better view. Sure enough and as proud as punch, Rusty trotted by the window. With that perky face, he almost grinned, and then ran to escape the clutches of his masters. It was a game. He jogged, dodged and evaded. Finally, Kevin leaped and engulfed him in a hug. Rusty licked Kevin's face, unaware of the trouble he was in.

"So, how did he get out front?" I asked.

Ray turned from the window, frowned and marched out

the back door. Kevin and Maria, with an armful of Rusty, entered the house. Maria scolded Rusty, "Bad boy. You aren't supposed to roam around." They hauled him to the backyard and I followed.

"Kevin, Rusty chewed through the wood fence back here. Look at this," Ray said, exasperated. He stood there, with his hands on his hips, as he swept one hand toward the gaping hole. "He worked fast. The fence is weak in spots and he found one. I have slats in the shed. Go get my hammer. It's in the toolbox."

Kevin stomped to the shed. I stayed back, away from my fuming husband, away from the destructive dog. In the meantime, Rusty played. He gamboled about the backyard and nudged another fence area. He growled, ready to chew some more. Maria corralled him and held on. It was all she could do to contain his puppy energy.

The sound of hammering echoed, and soon the fence was repaired. Ray attached a few extra pieces at other weak areas.

"Sorry, Dad," Kevin offered in a continuing string of apologies.

"Hey, obviously the fence had some issues. Let's get back in and finish dinner," his father answered, practically philosophical.

As we all entered the house, I noticed something amiss with my patio set. "Oh, wow, look at this chair." I pointed to one of our green-striped patio chairs that had now been ceremonially unstuffed. White cushion litter blew like cotton balls under the patio table. Suddenly I wasn't feeling quite so charitable.

Kevin hung his head. "Sorry, again and again."

Maria gave Rusty a swat and shoved his nose at the chair. "No, Rusty. Bad boy. Don't chew the chair cushions."

I was annoyed, but what could I do? He was a puppy in a strange area and he had lots of teeth to sharpen. At least he hadn't approached me to start gnawing. To be sure, I wasn't going to put an arm or hand near the Jaws of Death.

Kevin got the cage out and set it up. Seeing this, Rusty cowered and whimpered. He tried to dig in his heels and resist, but Kevin won. He found Rusty's toy bone which silenced his whining.

"One puppy wreaked havoc in less than an hour. What will happen when you have kids?" I asked.

"I doubt they'll chew through the fence," my stepson replied. Poor Kevin. He apologized again, and then poured a mug of margarita.

"So, after dinner, I'm taking Maria to visit my mom and sister. Then I've got some friends to see. We'll take Rusty with us. Unless, Joanne, do you want to baby-sit?"

Yeah, very funny. "No, thank you," was my answer.

We cleaned up dinner dishes while the kids prepared to leave. They came into the kitchen with Rusty on his leash. Rusty panted and tried to leap up on us, but Kevin jerked him back. "We're heading out. Thanks for dinner. I'm so glad to be back in Tex . . . oh no, Rusty! No!"

Rusty was piddling on the kitchen floor. Ray grabbed some paper towels for Kevin. Once again, Kevin apologized. "He never does this indoors—I swear."

"What time do you move to the apartment tomorrow?" I said, looking at the kitchen clock.

Realizing my patience had worn thin, Kevin replied, "Damn, maybe we should leave now and park the U-Haul outside their gate."

I patted him on the back. "You just gave me more evidence in case your dad ever decides he wants a dog. No, go have fun. Gonna be hot tomorrow. Moving at the end of May isn't the best timing."

They left and we shut the front door. I leaned against it, worn out from all the doggy bedlam.

"Holy crap, Ray. Are we gonna survive a Pit Bull staying in our guest room tonight?"

The Mighty Chicken Hunter

by
John Reas

I loved my German Shepherd, "Uhlie." He may have been the family dog, but all of my brothers and sisters understood he was "John's dog." Of course, with that tremendous honor came a great deal of responsibility, including feeding and cleaning up after Uhlie in his outside kennel area.

He may not have been allowed inside the house, but he did have a large doghouse, which I lined with old blankets to keep him warm during the winter months. And his enclosure in the side yard gave him plenty of room for running after the small rubber ball I used to play catch with him. The enclosure also became a natural meeting place for the neighbor kid. Being the king of Uhlie's domain, I would graciously allow them to come inside and hug on my dog from time to time. Uhlie thrived on the attention that often included a dozen children hugging and petting all at the same time.

However, it was somewhat difficult for a little guy like me to walk an 80-pound dog. This task my dad handled when he returned home from work. He'd grab the leash, snap it onto Uhlie's collar and walk him around the block before the family sat down for supper. I truly believe this ritual was one of Dad's simpler pleasures in life. He seemed to have a sense of fulfillment when walking the full-grown German Shepherd that he had purchased as a pup several years earlier.

Dad gave Uhlie his name. It was a nickname for Ulrich, and according to Dad, it was a good Teutonic name for such a fine dog. He said that Uhlie's namesake was a cantankerous old German who came over to the States after the war. I guess that was a sound enough reason to name the dog Uhlie. On the other hand, I would have chosen other, more impressive German names, such as Fritz, Max or Siegfried.

Uhlie was the kind of dog that rolled through life's ebbs and flows. Whenever I pretended to be Blondie from *The Good, The Bad and The Ugly* and practiced my cap pistol quick-draw on him, he took his assignment as being Angel Eyes from *The Good, The Bad and The Ugly* remarkably well and could play dead with the best of canines. If I practiced being Batman, Uhlie could always be counted on to be Robin, and never flinched whenever I attached his Boy Wonder cape to his collar, another demonstration of his versatility in the many roles I gave him.

Once, my parents decided to participate in the town's annual Halloween parade. In the small town of Defiance, Ohio, where I grew up, the Halloween parade was the kind of event everyone either participated in or witnessed. Dad and a neighbor placed Uhlie's doghouse on the back of a small trailer hitched to the family station wagon. Dad dressed up as Jed Clampett, my oldest sister, Mary, was Elly May, and my older brother, Bill, played Jethro. Even my grandma got into the act as Granny, sitting on her rocking chair, which was placed next to the doghouse. Mom drove *The Beverly Hillbillies* float while Uhlie had the best seat in the house as Jed's hound dog, sitting outside the doghouse while our neighbors and friends waved at them as they made their way down Clinton Street.

At Christmastime, during one of the rare moments the dog was allowed in the house, my sisters could be counted on to take leftover ribbons and bows and decorate him, transforming him into an overgrown hairy ornament. Sometimes, my sister, Cathy, entered his enclosure and dressed him up as if he was just another one of her Barbie dolls. Naturally, I would be outraged when I discovered this and would quickly take off the ridiculous costumes she had draped over him. Uhlie, on the other hand, didn't seem bothered by my sister's attempts at cross-dressing him. He accepted it with a great deal of equanimity as part of his responsibility in being the family pet.

But as a watchdog, Uhlie felt compelled to defend his turf against squirrels that encroached on our home. On the other side of Uhlie's enclosure was a great oak tree where my dad hung a tire swing. It also became a favorite location for a pair of squirrels. Whenever they appeared on the scene, Uhlie sprang into action and jumped up against the fence, barking himself hoarse until they were tired of torturing him with their presence and left. Although my parents took a rather dim view of Uhlie's outbursts concerning the squirrels, I was proud that my dog was being zealous in standing guard against such invaders. He was simply performing his canine duty with dignity and honor.

It was in this setting I experienced what was to become known in the Reas family lore as—*The Day of the Great Chicken Escapade.*

Every year around Easter, the G.C. Murphy five-and-dime store in downtown Defiance sold baby chicks. They were always a bestselling item the week before Easter as families brought them home as temporary pets. My friends usually had a couple they would keep for a while before their parents would adopt them out to a farmer in the area, never to be seen again. It was the type of event everyone looked forward to, along with decorating Easter eggs and attending the community egg hunts in the neighborhood park.

The year I turned 7, my parents decided it was time to also participate in the tradition. The week before Easter, they took us downtown to pick out our very own birds. When we arrived, we quickly found the area in the middle of the store where a large section had been cordoned off and filled with a teeming mass of bright-yellow baby chicks. We six kids stared in awe at the mass of chirping birds until we got down to the serious business of picking out those we wanted to claim as our own. "I'm naming mine Tabitha," chimed my sister Cathy, in a nod to one of her favorite television shows, *Bewitched.* Following her lead, I decided to name mine Agent 86 of *Get Smart* fame. The rest of my siblings quickly made their choices and Dad bundled the chicks in a cardboard box, paid for them at the cashier and we returned home.

Upon our arrival, Dad carried them into the garage where he had created a small coop made with chicken wire and lined with newspapers. A small spotlight had been set over the area providing both illumination and warmth for the feathered babies' new home. Mom tossed some chicken feed into the pen while all of us kids huddled around and observed them pecking at their food.

My other sister, Beth, who loved *The Monkees*, decided that four of the chicks should be named Davy, Peter, Michael and Micky in honor of the members of the pop group. This started a heated argument among her, Mary and Bill over naming-rights of the birds. Finally, Mom said, "Enough, kids. Let's go inside and wash up for dinner and let the babies get some rest. You can discuss what you want to name them later." With that, we trooped out of the garage and left them alone.

Throughout the week, we made repeated trips to the garage to look in on our chicks. My younger brother, Paul, became fond of the smallest one in the brood and would often gently pick it up and take it outside to show the other kids in the neighborhood. It was a peaceful time—all of us kids were home over spring break and engrossed by the wonder of having these small babies to occupy our attention.

On Easter Sunday, the family came home after service and had lunch before going outside. Dad was proud of his Leica M3 camera and had us gather around Mom's flower garden as he took the family photograph of us in our Easter garb. Earlier that morning, Mary, Beth and Mom had hidden Easter eggs around the yard and garden. The three of them had decorated many eggs the day before. And after the photography session,

Cathy, Bill, Paul and I went into the house to get our baskets for the egg hunt. Soon, the yard was a scene of controlled pandemonium as we scurried about searching for the brightly colored eggs while Dad snapped away with his camera.

After the hunt was over, Dad thought it would be a nice touch to bring the chicks out of the garage and let them wander about the yard under our supervision. He went into the garage, placed them in the cardboard box he'd brought them home in, brought them outside and released them into the yard. We watched with great enthusiasm as the babies explored their new surroundings. Once again, Dad captured it all on film. It was a perfect way to spend an Easter afternoon.

Shortly thereafter, Dad went into the house to put his camera away and Mom and my two oldest sisters returned to the kitchen to clean up the dishes. That left the four of us younger kids to keep an eye on the chicks while we counted the eggs we'd found. I looked over toward the side yard and noticed Uhlie sadly staring at me through the fence. I decided he needed some attention as well, so I went to his gate and opened it to give him a pat.

That was when the chaos began.

Demonstrating a speed and agility I never knew he existed, Uhlie jumped to his feet and barreled through the gate, making a beeline for the nearest chick. In seconds, the yard erupted into a scene of bedlam as Uhlie chased the little chicks, snapping and barking at the helpless birds. He stormed around the yard like an animal possessed while the babies scattered for the flower beds, bushes and the garden. Cathy broke out in tears while Bill tried to grab Uhlie's collar, but missed.

Paul was holding his special chick at the time and dropped it in the confusion—Uhlie turned, tried to snatch it and missed, his jaws closing on a bright yellow feather that fluttered to the ground. The rest of the family rushed out of the back door to witness the screams and Uhlie's berserk rampage.

"Uhlie, stop that!" yelled Mom. She was holding a kitchen broom and started to chase the dog around the yard. Cathy ran into the house, tears streaming down her face, and Paul wailed over the abrupt end of what had been a tranquil Easter afternoon.

The noise was such that neighbors poked their heads out of front doors to watch the show, as it had now spilled from the yard onto the street. Mom continued to chase Uhlie with the broom while Bill and my older sisters attempted to head him off. Hearing the commotion, other dogs in the neighborhood started a chain reaction of barking that brought more neighbors out to see what was happening. In the end, Dad tackled Uhlie, grabbed his collar and dragged him back into the enclosure. "John, WHAT were you thinking?!" he yelled at me, as my older sisters gathered up the chicks and glared at me in total contempt.

Needless to say, the chicks were sent to a neighboring farm the next day, never to be seen again. And that was the first and last time my parents ever attempted introducing chickens to our Easter celebrations.

As for Uhlie, his reputation only continued to grow as I recounted his mighty chicken exploits to my friends, embellishing his accomplishments every time I retold the story. Now if only he could get those pesky squirrels . . . .

Fighting Like Cats and Dogs

by

Cappy Hall Rearick

My dog, appropriately named "Tallulah Blankhead," born north of the Mason-Dixon Line without a rebel bone in her overweight body, went AWOL yesterday.

Our dog has an intellect rivaled only by garden tools. She has never left the backyard by herself. Why? Because she is obsessive-compulsive and has an attachment to three things: my husband, Babe, her food bowl and her favorite toy—a pale green stuffed rabbit appropriately named "Mr. Babe."

Yesterday, when I first missed her, I thought she had perhaps wandered onto the golf course next to our home in Georgia and got boinked in the head by an errant Titleist. But when I scanned the area as far as my eye could see there was no sign of her. I didn't even see a range ball.

Twenty minutes later, I was wringing my hands like a parent with a daughter out on her first date. If Tallulah had not always been such a lily-livered pooch who constantly hovered alongside her overprotective keepers, I would not have been concerned. But her disappearance was totally out of character. Maybe she was out on a first date.

I called for her until I was hoarse, with no results. I then shut up and listened for her incomparable Cockapoo *woof*. It took a while, but I finally heard it. The *woof* might as well have been miles away, but it sounded closer. My immediate reaction was that Tallulah Blankhead's obesity had put her in some kind of peril, so I shifted into high maternal mode.

I thought of sprinting like a roadrunner to the gun rack in order to show up at the rescue packing serious heat. But alas, I am a gun chicken. Tallulah, bless her enlarged little heart, was not born with that lily liver of hers—she got it from me. Instead of snatching an assault weapon, I grabbed the car keys. My mission? To rescue Babe's precious, dumber-than-a-box-of-hair, used-to-be-little pup.

Two blocks from the house, I spied our boxcar-lookalike dog. She was snarling at a fire hydrant. A few Southern patriots had painted the hydrant gray and white to resemble a corpulent Confederate soldier. I suppose our Yankee dog Tallulah Blankhead felt a call to arms, saw the painted hydrant and woofed herself into a war whoop.

I sat on the horn. "Tallulah Blankhead!" I yelled out of the window. Abruptly, she tore her eyes away from Robert E. Lee long enough to glance in my direction, puff up her chest, and then tear into General Lee as if he were drenched in *Eau de Alpo.*

"Hush your mouth, dawg, and get your fat ass in this car right now!" I yelled again, in what I thought was my most commanding voice. When she ignored me, I jumped out of the car, yanked her by the scruff of the neck and dragged her fat fluffy fanny into the back seat. To her credit, she had the grace to hang her head and look like a captured POW.

On the way home, I asked myself what might have caused her to stray from her obsessively natural habitat. Why had Babe's cowardly Cockapoo left the familiarity of hearth and home and deserted her post, only to get waylaid by a fire hydrant that was dressed to kill in Rebel Grey? Had the recently introduced meals for over-the-hill, overindulged, overweight canines not measured up to her epicurean palate? *What*, I wondered, *had lured Tallulah Blankhead into going AWOL?*

There are none so blind as those who will not see. The answer was right before my eyes.

It was "Sophie Sorrowful," the stray white kitten rescued from the clutches of the grim cat reaper. In only two weeks, she had managed to launch a *coup d'état*. Lord only knows what kind of propaganda she had been meowing in order to spark our dog's obvious rebellion. Armed with large blue eyes and saber-sharp teeth and nails, she came, she clawed, she conquered. Almost overnight, Sophie Sorrowful had snatched the throne away from Tallulah Blankhead in a bloodless coup to proclaim herself the Queen of Queens.

However, unlike General Lee, Tallulah did not surrender completely. Since the dawning of her freshly infused resolve while snarling at a fat fire hydrant, she had become more determined to stand her ground. For overweight Tallulah Blankhead that rebel fire hydrant corner was her Fort Sumter. Armed with newfound resolve and practicing a snarl, she quietly prepared to defend her formerly held position as Queen of the Hill.

This leads me to a quote I read recently by James Gorman: "Dogs tend to bravado. They're braggarts. In the great evolutionary drama, the dog is Sergeant Bilko, the cat is Rambo." If Tallulah Blankhead thought Sophie Sorrowful was ready to meet her Appomattox, she better think again—this cat-and-dog war ain't gonna be over till it's over.

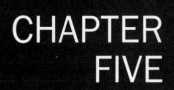

Dog Treats

Better than a box of Milk Bones!

The Great Escape

by
Sallie Wagner Brown

"Pepper" shivered as she struggled to keep her 19-pound, black, curly-haired, muscular body sitting still. She was only pretending she didn't care whether we came home or not.

It was after midnight, dark and cool on that moonless night in the forest surrounding our mountainside home in Western Oregon. Our neighbor fed Pepper dinner early in the evening, so she really needed to go outside. Nonetheless, she would never dream of letting us know that she needed us in any way, nor would she would forgive us for such shameful in-attention to her.

Pepper was so miffed at the delay that I had to coax her downstairs to the door leading to a large fenced area where she could run and relieve herself.

As she bumped down each step, lagging a little behind me, she snorted in such various tones that I'm sure I didn't want to know what she was saying in her own brand of dog-speak. As I opened the door to a patio covered by a deck above, she half growled and half barked a final comment, and then ran around the wall supporting the deck and under the tall old rhododendrons screening the yard from the patio.

I only had a moment to lean against the door frame and breathe in the mossy, rich fragrance of layers of bark dust, maple leaves and pine needles decomposing on the forest floor. Then a cougar screamed. Cold spikes pierced my stomach. I had heard a cougar once before in the backcountry of Idaho, but this one was in my front yard, only yards away on the other side of the wall of bushes—right in the area where Pepper had just wandered.

I called Pepper and started to run around the wall of bushes to chase the cougar away before he could get her. I realized just in time that I was outnumbered, even with just one cougar.

I shrieked for help. My husband, Butch, turned on outside lights from the upper deck as I threw folding lawn chairs, one after the other, in different directions over the bushes. Running out of furniture, I grabbed a water hose and sent jets of water randomly into the dark. I continued to yell for help. I tried to sound big and threatening.

I was desperate to scare the huge cat away before he noticed Pepper, or before Pepper noticed him! In the past, she has challenged everything from hissing wildcats to Bull Dogs and scared all of them off. She even stopped traffic in front of our driveway one time by facing down a Jeep Wrangler. I had to go pick her up, and even then she snorted and growled as the driver, laughing hysterically, waved and drove on. In my heart, I knew she would be bound to try to scare off even a mountain lion.

Just as my husband, unaware of our feline intruder, made it to the patio door, Pepper trotted around the bushes, onto the patio and into the house, still snorting—more put out at all the ruckus than being scared.

"I heard it! There was a cougar, there, out there! I threw stuff! Oh! She's OK, she's OK!" I tried to get my breath as I pulled my husband back into the house. Pepper trotted up the stairs to her bed in the kitchen.

"Are you sure?" Butch said. "Maybe it was a wildcat?"

"I heard it," I said, less certain now that Pepper was safely inside. I wanted to believe it wasn't a cougar, not in our yard! I laughed nervously and tried to smile as I went upstairs to sit by Pepper's bed and pet her, if she would let me. She was pretty mad at me.

I scratched her ears, and then ran my hand down the thick, black, curly fur of her back. She shivered. When I took my hand away, it was wet with blood. Looking more closely, I could see a puncture wound near her shoulder and another near her flank.

Seeing the blood on my hand, I called out for Butch. All he said when he saw the blood was, "Uh-oh," and then grabbed his car keys. I wrapped Pepper in an old beach towel. We knew the way to the 24-hour vet clinic on the other side of town very well.

Pepper tolerated the vet's exam, but she gave him the Miniature Schnauzer, fixed-eyed, death stare the entire time. He found two additional deep puncture wounds on the other shoulder and flank, but said that that no vital organs seemed to be involved. With hydrogen peroxide on the wounds and oral antibiotics, he said she should be fine.

I had to ask. "So it was probably a wildcat, right?"

"Absolutely not! With punctures that deep, in that configuration, it was definitely a cougar—and he had her!"

As we three stared at her wondering how she could have managed to escape, she snorted, shook her head, and then curled up on her towel. She moved her head so it barely touched my hand, and with a deep sigh, closed her eyes and drifted off to sleep.

Lost and Found

by
Janice Arenofsky

Murphy's Law—as it applies to dogs—decrees that mischievous things will only happen when Alpha Mom is on the phone, in the shower or otherwise occupied. A corollary to this is, the lower the probability of an event actually happening, the higher the price tag for the owner.

At first glance, the latest canine caper appeared more competitive than costly—you might even say a dog-eat-dog game of chess: two large canines circling the family chess board while two smaller dogs in the peanut gallery egged them on. The Collie appeared as if she were about to nose a chess piece to a more strategic location on the pink-and-white onyx board, while the yellow Lab marked time by thumping his tail obsessively as he deliberated his next rebuttal. Meanwhile, the two Schnauzers sent cryptic messages to each other with their eyebrows while the Maine

Coon, our sole cat, reported for her job as eyewitness.

When your animal family consists of four dogs and one cat, silence is usually a scarce commodity. When it lingers too long, worry becomes the operative word. So after several hours of unsolicited quiet, I peeked, suspiciously, out of my home office. Right away, I sensed something amiss. No bloody paw prints or broken lamps, but sure enough, one of the dogs had pushed past a 3-foot-high, heavy cardboard barrier I had erected to block them from the living room. My longtime fail-safe security measure had let me down.

It wasn't a pretty sight. Our chess board remained on the coffee table, but chess pieces littered the carpet as if a band of robbers had ransacked the room. When I finally mustered the courage to assess the damage, I saw the usual suspects gazing back at me with their all-too-familiar goofy grins. As if in a police lineup, they endeavored to deflect blame onto the other guy. Heads pivoting, legs shuffling back and forth, they struggled to look noncommittal. But I knew from past experience that appearances could be deceiving. The ho-hum attitude was a blatant attempt at denial. They knew the living room was off limits—hadn't I read the riot act to them several times already?

What with their records of past crimes, I was sorely tempted to throw the book at them—dispense with a trial of their peers, invoke the three-times-you're-out law and sentence them to life in the slammer. A daily diet of kibble and water—no biscuits or cookies for those rascals—sounded about right. But first, I would prolong their agony a bit and investigate the crime scene. Like any other television CSI professional, I ascertained that except for the chess set (obviously torn asunder by a tsunami), the only visible damage was the ton of multicolored dog hairs pasted onto the furniture.

An hour later, I was still searching. Except for discovering some old newspapers squashed beneath the sofa cushions and a few Tootsie Roll wrappers, I was slowly getting nowhere in my investigation. Plus, my activities were beginning to resemble housework—something I did reluctantly, if at all.

It was then I had an epiphany—of sorts. The problem was not what the accused felons had left behind, but rather what they had absconded with. I knew enough about the game of chess to deduce that the white rook was missing and unaccounted for. In what I hoped was my best law enforcement and politically correct voice, I asked, "OK, which one of you critters was nutty enough to ingest a chess piece?"

"Chauncey," the Lab, was the most likely candidate. His 9-month-old rap sheet already stretched several leash-lengths long, warning of an inherited tendency to devour everything in sight. At current count, he had chewed several ballpoint pens, gnawed through two lawn sprinkler heads and wolfed down a pair of raw chicken breasts. And that was just in one week. The word *mischievous* did not do him justice.

So needless to say I wound up in my vet's waiting room at 5 P.M. on that Friday night, awaiting the results of X-rays. While leafing through an old copy of *Cat Fancy*, I was imagining the worst: emergency surgery to the tune of several thousand dollars. Meanwhile, the dog was throwing himself a pity party. With his hindquarters tucked under my chair and his paws propped under his head, he looked as if some bully of a

Great Dane had come along and swiped his best bone. A closer observation revealed my Lab puppy was really a study in contrasts. Although his eyes said, "Help, I'm a prisoner of my own stupidity," his mouth seemed frozen in an impish smile, as if boasting of rare accomplishments.

"Wait until you see this," I heard the vet say in an amazed tone from the back of his office. In my haste to confront the consequences of Chauncey's latest crime, I nearly tripped over my prisoner. An 11" x 14" image of the canine digestive tract illuminated the room. Toward the bottom of the X-ray, in what I took to be Chauncey's stomach, I could discern the unmistakable outline of a miniature castle. Sure enough, there was the missing rook. Without medical intervention, I knew my 60-pound pup could not eliminate the imported hand-carved chess piece.

"What do we do now?" I asked weakly.

Looking at my ghostly pale face, the vet could tell I was in no shape to deal with a four-figure surgical procedure, followed by a lengthy recuperation with a young active patient. "I think we can get him to barf it up," he said, with a devilish smile.

Fifteen minutes later, I, too, was chuckling. Thanks to the wonders of fast-working emetics, the accused had taken responsibility for his crime and confessed. He probably did not feel any better for it, but I certainly did. At $125, divesting the cat—no—dog burglar of his take was a real bargain. Besides, law and order had prevailed.

Standing behind the reception room counter waving the bill, the veterinary technician resembled a trial judge about to rap her gavel. Smiling, she handed over the recently recovered chess piece, which I hurriedly jammed into my pocket. I mumbled, "Case closed."

As my faithful friend and I exited through the double doors, I thought once again of Murphy's Law and other everyday axioms, such as the fallacious, "lightning-doesn't-strike-twice" one. That's when I knew tomorrow I'd be making a pink-and-white chess set deposit at Goodwill. Call it crime prevention.

Janice and Chauncey

Special Delivery

by
Jerry W. Davis, DVM

Immediately after graduating from veterinary school in 1966, I entered the Air Force and was sent to a base in North Carolina. Since I was in a medical field, I was assigned to the base hospital and directly supervised by the hospital commander, who happened to be an obstetrician. He was the officer who wrote and forwarded my annual officer performance report to the Wing Commander for endorsement. Needless to say, that report would determine my future promotion potential. Thus, I felt a bit of pressure to perform well.

After a hospital staff meeting one day, the commander told me that his family dog, "Missy," a Miniature Dachshund, had been bred by his neighbor's dog. Missy was obviously pregnant, for her belly was growing rapidly. He was concerned because the neighbor's dog, "Joey," was a Basset Hound and much larger than his little Dachshund.

"Yes, that doggy romance occurred in our backyard," the

commander told me.

"Wow!" I replied. "That must've been a sight to behold!"

"We didn't witness the encounter that night. But as we let Missy back into the house, we saw Joey leaving our backyard. He crawled under the fence between our houses, and there was a definite sheepish expression on his face!"

Being an OB/GYN doctor, my boss knew that a serious obstetrical problem might occur when Missy was ready to deliver. He had several questions for me. As a relatively inexperienced DVM, I explained everything I had learned in school, hoping that I remembered correctly. I told him that the puppies should be ready for delivery 58 to 63 days after the romantic encounter. I suggested that he watch Missy closely during that time. If she went into labor for more than a couple of hours without giving birth, he should call me.

I had not performed a Caesarian section since graduation, so I began to review the procedure from my old notes and books I'd used in college. After all, my boss had performed many sections on humans and he would probably be looking over my shoulder during Missy's surgery. Wow—talk about pressure for this young inexperienced veterinary officer. My career weighed in the balance if Missy couldn't deliver the puppies by herself.

Well, it happened. My boss called at 11 P.M. soon after to tell me Missy had been straining for almost two hours.

"No pups!" he said. I told him to meet me at my office in 15 minutes.

I didn't have time to call one of my sergeants for assistance, so I asked my wife, Marilyn, to go with me to assist. When we arrived at my veterinary clinic 10 minutes after the call, my boss was already there waiting for us. He carried Missy inside and placed her on the surgery table. While sweat formed on my brow, Marilyn and I prepared the little dog for my first solo Caesarian section.

After I administered sedation and local anesthesia, Marilyn shaved, washed and sterilized Missy's belly. I donned a surgical gown, mask and gloves. Marilyn opened the sterilized surgical instrument pack and I picked up the scalpel and began the incision. Missy's belly was so swollen and tight that it reminded me of cutting a ripe watermelon, where the surface rips ahead of the knife.

As I opened the uterus, a puppy's head was exposed.

"Wow! That's a big puppy!" exclaimed my boss, who had also put on a surgical mask.

"Yes, and there are several more in there," I answered.

One at a time, I handed eight puppies to Marilyn, who cleaned them and placed them in a warm blanket until they could be given to Missy.

"Should I perform a spay while I'm in here?" I asked my boss.

There was no hesitation in his answer. "Absolutely! I don't want to go through this again."

So I removed Missy's uterus and ovaries, completed the surgery and all three of us were relieved and smiling. Since Missy was only sedated, not asleep, she seemed to have an expression of gratitude on her face as well. The entire procedure had gone perfectly.

We weighed Missy after the surgery—and much to our

surprise, she weighed less than the total weight of the puppies.

The next day, I went to see Missy's suitor, Papa Joey. I patted his head, thinking, *You sly dog!* However, if it hadn't been for that big guy, the opportunity for me to show off my skills would not have happened.

I'm happy to report that my next officer performance report was outstanding, and I was promoted the following spring!

It's Elementary

by
Marsha Porter

When my neighbor's daughter turned 13, her mom took her to the pound to get her the dog she'd always wanted. The darling Terrier—whom they named "Scruffy"—was a cross between Benji in a gray coat and Toto from *The Wizard of Oz*. Sadly, his arrival was a bit late in life for the budding teenager. I saw her walk Scruffy all of two times before replacing him and his leash with first a portable house phone and then her own cell.

The lack of attention from Scruffy's adolescent mom led to a series of escapes by the scraggly little pooch. His accessibility to freedom came via unlatched gates, opened garage doors and the ever-popular front door, which was held ajar to greet visitors, repairmen and door-to-door pests. His dart to explore the great outdoors would typically be followed by shouts from either the teen drama queen or her mother. Rescue attempts by Scruffy's owners didn't include chasing him and bringing him home. I, however, repeatedly went after the energetic fellow. When I'd get within earshot of the little runaway, I'd bend down and invite him to come to me. He trotted happily to me every time for a pat and ride home in my arms.

Needless to say, Scruffy and I became fast friends. Sometimes, when I spied him exploring the street when his owners weren't home, I'd take him in and open a can of food, which he wolfishly inhaled.

Five years passed with Scruffy getting progressively less attention from his owners. Suddenly, a "For Sale" sign appeared on my neighbor's lawn. I learned they were moving to an apartment that didn't allow pets. Concerned, I asked, "What about Scruffy?"

"We'll take him back where we got him," my neighbor answered.

"But you got him from the pound."

"Well, he's so cute. I'm sure he'll get adopted again," she responded.

Since he was no longer a puppy, I was pretty sure of Scruffy's fate if he were returned to the pound. I began to think of my hyper Jack Russell Terrier whom I had named "Watson," wondering if the two of them would get along should Scruffy come to live with us.

With a week before the move, Scruffy was getting out more often than ever. It seemed like the gate and garage door were constantly open now. I asked my neighbor if Scruffy could stay at my house while she was moving. In the back of my mind, I was secretly hoping Scruffy and Watson would become fast friends. The neighbor happily agreed.

When the two canines met, they eyed each other, nose to nose. One of them must have yipped "tag," because they began chasing each other around the backyard, stopping only for brief rolls or rests on the lawn. My non-stop, action-oriented Jack Russell had finally met his match. The two became an instant Olympic-level relay team that day, and friends, as well.

By midweek, I assured my neighbor that Scruffy was welcome to make his permanent home with me, instead of being dropped off at the pound. She seemed relieved and once again agreed. Later that day, she brought over a half-empty bag of dog food, which was designed for large breed dogs.

"This is Scruffy's food. We got it when we adopted him. He doesn't eat much," she informed me.

I thanked her and asked her to leave it there, on my front porch. After she left, I looked inside the bag and saw giant chunks meant for a Saint Bernard, not a 17-pound Terrier. A number of tiny bugs had also taken up residence inside in what had to be at least 5-year-old kibble. I promptly bagged the entire thing in plastic and disposed of it.

When I took Scruffy to my vet, I was not surprised to find out he was underweight and had bad teeth. Eleven of his teeth had to be pulled, leaving him with a softened mouth and an adorable uneven grin. Now he only eats wet food, but he eats it with gusto and has gained 6 pounds.

I thought I'd also have a problem with Scruffy running off to explore, since he'd made such a career of it when he lived next door. Surprisingly, he has never tried. Now, whenever I open a can of food or simply say his name, Scruffy rewards me with an upturned grin and eager wag. With all the love he could want, plenty of food to eat and Watson as his companion, Scruffy has decided to stay. To him, it's elementary.

Scruffy

Watson

Sentry of the Homestead

by
Kathleene Baker

The year was 1924. With supper finished, my Grandpa Boucher gathered table scraps and headed outside. He called and whistled but his Collie didn't respond. Worry set in— "Shep" was always on the back step, awaiting tasty morsels.

"Have you kids seen Shep? He never misses dinner scraps," Grandpa hollered through the screen door to the family. No one— not his six children or Grandma—had seen him since noon.

In search of Shep, Grandpa passed the cellar and heard a faint whimper. He found Shep in the cellar, moaning. Then he realized Shep had been bitten by a venomous snake. His right front leg was badly swollen and fiery red.

The family grabbed a fresh pan of water, some food and blankets, all of which was carried down the cellar steps. Shep was gently placed upon the soft bedding, but refused food or drink. Grandpa spoke to him affectionately, stroked his beautiful head, and wiped at a lone tear before leaving his beloved

Shep for the night. From the day he'd brought the tiny pup home, their bond was unique. It was hard for him to see his dog like this.

Grandpa faithfully checked on Shep, encouraging food and drink, but Shep refused. After 12 hours, Grandpa gently opened the dog's mouth and dribbled water from his fingertips. The procedure was repeated numerous times daily, along with wrapping the infected leg with cool, wet rags to control swelling. Coal oil was applied to the actual bite using a chicken feather, for the slightest touch was excruciating to Shep. After five days, Shep lapped at warm oatmeal Grandma had prepared and took his first drink of water. Loving eyes bore into Grandpa as if to say, "I'm doing my best to hang on . . . don't give up."

On the tenth day, Grandpa let go with whoops of excitement as Shep emerged from the cellar, hungry for dinner scraps. On the mend, Shep returned to his normal evening ritual—lazing next to Grandpa's chair, head resting atop his owner's foot. And bedtime found him sleeping on a pallet in my grandparents' bedroom. With tender care, young Shep made a complete recovery.

Shep was a valued asset on the dairy farm, due to his flawless herding instincts. He was a strong and brilliant canine, devoted to the entire family. As six children roamed the countryside hunting, fishing or exploring, my grandparents never worried with Shep at their side.

Come spring, Shep supervised crops being planted. One crisp morning, Charlie, one of the teenage sons, began sowing kaffir corn. It was an arduous task, handling a team of four workhorses and a single row planter. Shep wandered occasionally, searching hedge rows for rabbits in need of a good chase.

By late morning, the temperature had risen considerably. Charlie stopped the workhorses under a tree, near some bags of seed. He tossed his jacket atop one bag and plopped down for a brief rest. Shep lay beside him, nudging Charlie's hand for ear rubs. They both dozed briefly until awakened by a clanging bell—the noon meal was ready.

When Charlie reached for his jacket, Shep clamped down on his arm, pulling him in the opposite direction. Charlie knew it was not an attempt to play. He inched forward slowly, but Shep then placed himself between the boy and his jacket.

"OK. You're telling me something is wrong with my jacket. I understand now."

Shep whined as Charlie gently lifted one edge of his jacket upward. He heard it before he saw it; beneath lay a coiled-up rattlesnake, tail quivering and tongue flicking the air! Charlie backed away cautiously, as did Shep. "Good boy! Good boy, Shep!" They raced to the farmhouse, collapsed in the shade of a cottonwood tree and had a lively wrestling match to celebrate Shep's vigilance.

On the south Kansas plains, long before it was customary for dogs to be considered family members, Shep held that very distinction. He became part of the family the moment Grandpa held the tiny pup in one hand and gazed into his enchanting eyes. In return, Shep became a staunch protector of Grandpa's family and, most importantly, sentry of the homestead.

Buddy's Pride

by
Betty Keel

Coming home late from work, my husband and I never knew what we would find in the darkness of our driveway. On one occasion, a coiled 4-foot rattlesnake greeted us on the walkway. Another time, an alligator stretched all 9 feet of his body out on our driveway as if to say, "Welcome home!"

Yet not all of our surprises were ghastly. One of our dearest discoveries was a small black Labrador Retriever crouched timidly in a corner of the garage.

After years of serving in the military and living in crowded cities all over the world, my husband retired and we settled on my mother's old home place, bringing with us our son, his cat "John Wayne," a dog called "Ben," and our eclectic mismatch of belongings, along with our commitment to be part of a civilian community. We treasured the opportunity to make a new life in an old farmhouse in the middle of a 32-acre pasture,

25 miles away from any hint of city life. However, we learned quickly that country life had its advantages and disadvantages. For certain, living in a place surrounded by fields and forests availed one's dwelling to becoming a magnet for all kinds of animals seeking refuge, and our home was no exception.

Soon after we settled into our surroundings, I accepted a job teaching at a local university, while my husband became an administrator at a nearby college. Both jobs required long hours away from home. However, in our spare time, we landscaped our yard, erected fences and established gates that remained open as a welcomed gesture.

Inside our gates, a new family atmosphere emerged. I was content to be back in my element as we became more attuned to nature. A family of red foxes, a flock of wild geese, and many deer, rabbits and raccoons all became part of our lives. Likewise, the night offered a whole trilogy of eerie alto, soprano and tenor sounds, signaling wildlife activity in the pine thickets stretching across the back field. We became accustomed to those sounds, deeming them acceptable as long as they kept their distance. Our neighbors passed the word that we didn't hunt, didn't trap, but did take in destitute animals, which led to many surprises for us.

One night, we came home to discover a Siamese kitten on our doorsteps, which we named "Mooch." Next came a Calico Manx, followed by a long-haired Ragdoll cat (pregnant of course!) which we named "Jitterbug." And there were others, including this canine gift that appeared in our garage on the coldest night of the year.

We had braced for a freezing night as we each pulled into

the garage after work. Exiting our vehicles, we heard whimpering and traced it to a dark corner. Crouched in the shadows was a black Labrador Retriever, 10 months old at best, shivering from cold and fright. Mud caked his black coat, and his sad eyes revealed possible abuse. That night, he became our "Buddy."

Lo and behold, on that same evening, Buddy's brother was dropped off at our cousin's house nearby. It was obvious both young dogs were suffering from mange.

Buddy enjoyed a feast that night, followed by a warm bath the next day before his trip to the veterinarian. Serious negotiations about his future ensued the following night after work. To put the evening's discussion into a formula of which Einstein himself would have approved, it goes something like the following:

Einstein's Theory of Dog-Catitude: DG1 + CT7 = TRBL8
Translation: *Just how well would Buddy and our seven "outside" cats get along?*
Our formula for the final decision: WT & C
Translation: *Wait and See*

Buddy adapted well into his new family. He trusted us unconditionally as he realized we would not abuse him. As time progressed, he established his own rules, probably based on prior experiences. He would not go into a pen, and if forced, he would collapse into a dead faint. Consequently, he roamed freely in our yard and even today, 10 years later, he will not leave our yard unless we walk with him. He marks his spots every morning and will allow no other dogs entry. Buddy also will eat his meals only if my husband or I stand there watching.

We jokingly accused him of creating his own job description and a list of do's and don'ts while we are at work, including his watching after our feline family.

One morning, hearing Buddy barking fiercely, I ran outside to find two wild dogs near the barn. I screamed at them because that was where Jitterbug had her kittens. Saddened in my heart, I found Jitterbug dead, along with two of her kittens. I looked frantically for the third kitten, with Buddy beside me, and I returned several times to search. Just before nightfall, Buddy scratched on the door, and I went out to find the third kitten lying on the step. It was still wet from Buddy's mouth and was having a seizure. True to the nature of his breed, Buddy brought the kitten ever so gently to me. Inside, I wiped it, wrapped it in a blanket, and held it, thinking it was dead. Noticing movement, I removed the blanket to find the kitten alive! I named him "Trickster," for obvious reasons.

As Buddy and Trickster grew up together, they became inseparable, and still are. Trickster is the only cat that Buddy will allow on his front porch pad. They snuggle together each night. Most of the time, Buddy can be found on the front porch, allowing no one near the front door unless we pat his head, indicating it is all right. Not only is Buddy our protector, he also reigns supreme over our pride of cats. Or should I say *his* pride of cats?

The first time I saw Buddy grooming Trickster, I nearly fainted, thinking he was biting her. In truth, Buddy was taking mincing, gentle bites across Trickster's back to remove fleas— the same way he fleas and grooms himself. For the last seven years, Buddy has groomed Trickster and our entire cat fleet.

They stand in line to take their turns—with the exception of two who have no desire to be groomed, making it abundantly clear by slapping his face with their paws.

Buddy and Trickster have bonded for life. Buddy has severe arthritis now and experiences difficulty getting up and down, yet with great pride, he walks his fence line daily, guarding us like a champ. He meets and greets us every evening, and we reciprocate by giving him snacks kept in our cars. The cats adore Buddy for his gentle love expressions and affectionate looks, but most of all for his grooming skills. Max Eastman in *Enjoyment of Laughter* said that dogs "laugh with their tails," and if that is true, then Buddy has laughed often since we made him our pride and joy, on that cold, wintry night.

Buddy and Trickster

We All Shine On

by
Dennis C. Bentley

I climbed into the car Saturday morning to meet with some friends. My wife was busy with dog-training classes and working on evaluations for the local rescue kennel where she volunteered. I decided the day would be greatly improved if I stopped and picked up some real coffee. I could go out of my way to the quick-gas place for their dark-roast blend, but Hardees made some almost as good. Hillsboro doesn't have a Starbucks—that's how small and rural Hillsboro is.

There was a wait at the Hardees' counter as an old gentleman in overalls separated, dug and carefully counted out lint-covered change. I couldn't justify impatience—I had plenty of time.

While waiting, I noticed folks at the tables pointing out the big window. One of them said something about a dog, while others just shook their heads.

As I capped my steaming Joe, I headed toward the door and spotted the pup. A long, low-slung Dachshund dutifully marched down the grassy median between the eatery and the road, heading directly toward the busy intersection. I stepped out, looked around and saw no one in pursuit or calling out.

The dog was wearing a collar—I could make out tags dangling almost to the ground. The rust-colored wiener dog continued to trot confidently toward the highway. I could tell that he was not road-trained since the heavy traffic seemed to be of no interest to him whatsoever. He was not aware of the danger. This was someone's baby boy, an indoor pup.

I couldn't just drive away. I couldn't just hope or pray for the best. I was at this place and time and was the dog's only hope for life, even if he didn't know it yet.

I've chased loose dogs many times and I've worked with rescues and fosters for over 10 years. The knowledge you pick up after doing this dozens of times is that to chase is to fail. You simply must be more interesting and appealing to the dog than whatever is currently motivating it. I had no chunks of meat or bread on me, so I was left with only myself as a lure.

I needed a leash. Though the dog was small, a threatened or frightened dog was not something you wanted to hold onto for very long. It occurred to me that I could fashion a leash out of the canvas strap from my book bag. I unclipped it and made a slip-loop at one end. A loop is much easier to get around a dog's neck than trying to clip onto the dog's collar, and safer, too. You won't be bitten.

I approached the little dog and at first he paid me no notice. As I got closer, I sensed the flight-or-fight response building in him, his eyes shifting rapidly from me to the road, me, the road, me, the growling diesel truck and back to me.

Now about 8 feet away, I dropped to my knees, slapped the front of my thighs with my hands and dropped my head as if greeting a Japanese host. If you watch dogs interact, you will recognize the movement. When wanting to play, a dog will drop to its front elbows and slap its paws on the floor. This is an instinctual dog-play indicator, a movement that indicates, "No harm intended—let's just wrestle for fun!"

The dog picked up on it and stopped looking toward the intersection. Interested, curious, but unsure—it was a stalemate! I was reluctant to approach; if he suddenly became frightened his only escape would be into the road—I would rather he simply stayed where he was, for as long as he needed, than for him to dash toward certain death.

I could see the collar and tags clearly. The collar was bright and clean, and there were two tags dangling, one still shiny. This was certainly someone's beloved pooch—clean, healthy coat, clean teeth and new tags. A small Dachshund is usually an indoor dog. In this downtown location, to me it meant a dog that probably was walked frequently. I knew that walks are the acme of a day for house dogs. Even the luckier dogs that have fenced yards to freely roam still love being leashed up and led around the block. Fascinating and exciting new sights and smells abound, as do chances to read and leave pee-mail on trees and mailbox posts.

Suddenly, I knew how to get his attention. I showed him the leash. Still on my knees, I held it out and just let it dangle in front of me. It worked! He wanted to walk. His learned reaction to the visual stimulus of a leash was going for a walk. For that moment, I might as well have been offering him a slab of peanut-butter-covered raw meat with bone-marrow sprinkles.

He came right to me. I dropped the makeshift lasso around his neck and gently cinched it. He didn't resist at all. I stood up, led him away from the road and back toward the grassy area behind the drive-thru. He was as happy as a clam and took to the makeshift leash like he had just inherited a fortune.

Once we had bonded for a few minutes, I sat at the curb and drew him close. I checked for injuries; there were none apparent. I rubbed his soft, furry head and he characteristically rolled over and offered me his ample belly. I accepted this great gift and we were soon the best of friends.

The tags were both vet-issued vaccination tags, no personal ID with the dog's name or home address. I fished out my phone and dialed the number on the shiniest tag.

A lady answered and I told her the situation. She asked for the tag number.

"Oh, that's Oscar, he's a sweetie," she cooed.

"Yes, ma'am, he seems to be just that."

"Well, he belongs to Frank Whitman, his phone number is . . ."

I stopped her. "Wait, I don't have a pen on me." I hoped she would offer to call Frank herself, but she didn't.

"Well, I do have his address," she offered instead.

I looked around at the street signs, assuming the short-legged little beast probably hadn't ventured far. "Great, read it off to me, and I'll try to find it."

"OK. It's P.O. Box 354 . . ."

"Hold on ma'am, I wasn't planning to mail the pooch home—is there a street address?"

"No, I'm afraid not."

"Well, let me go to my car so I can write down the phone number." I got to the car, opened the door and Oscar happily jumped into the passenger seat and readied himself for a ride. Finding pen and paper, I told the lady to go ahead. She read off the number, I thanked her, disconnected and dialed Oscar's home.

"Is this Frank?" I asked the heavy male voice.

"Yeah, I'm Frank."

"Sir, I have something of yours. I'm told that his name is Oscar."

"Oscar? Oh no, he got out? Dad-burn it, I saw him here just a few minutes ago."

"He's fine sir, he was wandering around the Hardees' parking lot."

"Well, that's great. Don't know how he got out though. I'll send my boy right down there. What kind of car you in?"

I looked around at the 10 or so vehicles in the lot, most of them small silver cars. I decided to go a different route. "I'll be the man walking your dog," I answered. He said that would work and thanked me again.

Oscar and I walked to the grass again. A moment later, I looked up to see a mid-40ish, lanky, near-toothless man approaching us with a big genuine smile.

"There you are, Oscar!" he said. I unclipped my book bag strap and the man picked up the now-ecstatic pup. "I sure do thank you, sir," the man said, his face being slobbered upon by the carefree dog.

"No problem at all, just happy to help."

I went on to my meeting feeling rather good about myself. Unlike my lovely wife, I'm no dog expert. But just being around her has taught me lots of things about dogs. I knew that I was perfectly prepared for just such a situation without even being consciously aware of it.

The meeting let out at noon. The heat advisory warnings had been accurate—the pavement outside the library had turned into a flat-top griddle. I approached my car and thought something didn't look quite right. As I got closer, it dawned on me; it was the rear-view mirror, which was dangling by a wire. The glue holding it to the windshield had melted. I opened the car door, the blast of intense heat nearly knocking me over. The glue spot on the windshield was still tacky.

Not a major problem, not cancer or a death in the family or losing a job, but still, yet another unexpected minor chore had been tossed into my lap.

Where's the karma? I thought. I had gone out of my way and rescued a beloved pet and asked for absolutely nothing in return! Cosmic justice owed me just a little something. Do I find a five-spot on the sidewalk? *Do I get a call from a long-lost friend? No—my mirror melts!*

Then I realized something important about karma and rescuing Oscar—I'd do it over again without giving it a second thought. I didn't need a reward. Just knowing I made someone's life a little less tragic was all I needed to feel worthy. I'll never cure cancer or solve global warming, but hey, today I saved a family's dog.

That was karma enough for me, and for Oscar.

Love Me,
Love My Dog

by
Marnie Frances

My dog of 16 years is a funny little critter. He isn't a specific breed, just small, black, has a white bib with a singular ermine spot placed within it, hard crunchy triangular ears and small buggy eyes. Height-wise, he barely even reaches the bottom of my kneecaps. His name is "Fizz," amongst other variants, and he is my best friend.

My dearest little Fizzbomb, day and night, stays by my side, to the point where not only does he sleep with me on "his" half of the bed, it is said that we share the same expressions in every photo of us together. At the time I laughed, but on reflection, it made me worry a little because I was not too sure that I wished to be seen as crunchy-eared and buggy-eyed.

Naturally, when my little Fizzcake met the "Partner," he was overcome with jealously and not at all impressed at the prospect of having to give up his half of the bed. In defiance, he attempted to make it as awkward and as difficult as possible for said Partner to get into the bed, to move Fizzpeep even an inch, to sort out the duvet or to curl up with me. He achieved all of this by purposely turning himself into dead weight with no intention of moving.

On one occasion, in the middle of the night I was awakened by a vast amount of muttering and cursing. Fizzmunch had an attitude and wanted to get on the bed and sleep in his very own spot! I awoke to Partner sitting up, holding his head in his hands. I was soon informed that the mutt had been at it for hours and wouldn't let him sleep. Fizz jumped on and off the bed and whimpered endlessly from various spots around the room.

As if on cue, Fizzpip jumped onto the bed and stuck his muzzle in my Partner's despairing face, whining, snorting and generally being as irritating as possible. His cold nose brushed my Partner's nose, due to the way that his little round head snaked side to side when wagging his tail in delight. He was enthralled by the fact that, once again, he was being presented with the prime opportunity to annoy Partner.

Don't get me wrong, I love my Partner, but I'd had my dog for 13 years.

"I HATE YOU!" he cried down the dog's nostrils before huffing, puffing, grunting and stomping his way into the spare room to sleep.

Fizzle soon settled in the warm patch next to me with a smug expression, for he finally had exactly what he wanted. Almost instantly, he began to snore.

The next morning, a grumpy, sleep-deprived Partner returned and pulled back the covers to see Fizz fast asleep, with his paws upon my back. I rolled over and scooped my Fizzball up, giving him a cuddle as we both looked up at Partner morosely.

"You're horrible, you are, saying that to my Fizzcake last night," I said in a reprimanding voice to Partner.

"Well, he's horrible!"

"No, he's not!" I replied, cradling my dog like a newborn child. "Love me—love my dog!"

Fizz and Marnie

Rubik's Dog

by
Frank Ramirez

They say it's important to exercise our minds as well as our bodies if we want to remain fit as a fiddle. Considering the shape of some fiddles I've seen, I'm not sure it's much of a goal.

You remember the Rubik's Cube? It was a 1980's craze. The cube had six multicolored sides and each side twisted and turned on its own axis. With six different colors, the goal was to arrange things so each of the six sides was a single color.

It was supposed to be an intelligence test. I remember it was pretty simple to get one side a single color, and maybe two. After that, it got harder. It was easy to obsess over the thing.

One day, magically, after a few twists and weeks of effort, everything fell into place—I had solved the Rubik's Cube. Six sides of solid colors. I proudly placed my accomplishment on the shelf, mute proof of my cleverness. That is, until some busybody picked it up and started twisting and turning until the whole thing was ruined.

After that, I bought one of the books that showed how to solve the puzzle. Through a series of quickly executed twists and turns, I was soon able to resolve the cube in a minute or less. Once I knew the secret, it never produced the same satisfaction compared to a combination of willpower, cleverness and abstruse luck to put that cube into shape.

The cube always came to mind whenever I watched someone else approach any kind of puzzle with the same cleverness and determination I had used in solving the cube's riddle. This comparison happened one sunny day while standing in front of our kitchen window. I happened to look out back and saw our dog Kit in absolute concentration. Unbeknownst to me at the time, Kit would soon become known as "Rubik's Dog."

Kit is half Lab, half Golden Retriever. There's not much golden to her. Instead, she's black from tail to nose except for one white spot on her body. But her brain was always working! Slowly, even for a dog, but it was working. Her brow would furrow when she stared at a problem. I always thought she was hoping to stare her way through the difficulty.

In recent weeks, Kit has become entranced with the plastic compost heap we have in the back ard. It's up against the corner along the fence line. It has brown plastic walls with a lid, and inside are decomposing orange peels, potato skins, cabbage leaves, carrot tops, green tea bags (no staples, no papers), coffee grounds, sunken squash, lettuce six degrees beyond wilted, jicama that we've plain forgotten, asparagus butts, cauliflower ends, greens and beans and things dumped from tureens. It's all there, just falling apart, creating a tremendous amount of internal heat, even in winter.

The compost is alive. Bugs live there. Bacteria thrive. Mice hang out and have litters. And Kit knows it. She haunts that compost heap. She circles it, sniffing and digging and pawing, letting the mice know she is on to them.

Kit began to dig a deep trench between the compost and the fence, right past roots, past rocks and nearly a foot deep. To her, it was a science project. It was a dream. It was a vision. There's drive here. Kit dug, stepped back to check her progress, and dug again. I figured out that sooner or later, she'd dig under the fence to freedom. Either that or the whole compost heap would fall into the trench!

Something had to be done. However, the dog was smarter than me. I was stumped. How do I stop a dog with that amount of determination? So I went to an expert—my wife. She could outthink a dog and she could certainly outthink me. I described the problem to Jennie and she had an answer pretty quick—take some logs from the burn pile and stack them in the trench.

Would that work? I thought. Doing as instructed, I placed three logs inside Kit's trench. Then I stepped back. Kit, who was watching me, stood stock still, staring down into her trench. Something was different! She realized it now was impossible to dig.

I walked back into the house and looked at Kit from 30 yards away. She stood there, not moving, for several minutes. Finally, she dropped to a seated position, and then a lying position, never taking her eyes off those logs. She was stumped. She became a Rubik's Dog, on a quest to solve this new puzzle.

I felt sorry for her, having taken her fun away. Kit, however, had no time for self-pity, as far as I could see. She was presented with a new challenge and she intended to be every bit the equal of it.

It took two days. Two days in which she spent every moment we gave her outside, whether rain or snow, looking at and through the logs in the trench. Clouds rolled in from the west, the sky turned from blue to gray to black, and still she studied.

At last, the light bulb moment! Kit stepped away from the trench and began to dig a hole! A hole next to the trench. It was an elegant solution, simple and effective. This time, Jennie didn't wait for me to discover it or ask for her guidance. She simply took an old gate from an abandoned dog fence and laid it over Kit's newly-dug hole.

Now you could see the smoke from Kit's brain and her ears standing straight out from her skull as she considered this new setback. There was no anger on her part, no accusatory stares. Just puzzlement.

She's still out there, gazing at the hole underneath the old fence gate. The compost still crumbles, decomposing to its own inverted melody, providing sustenance to generations of bacteria, insects and mice, before the final product is folded into the soil to nourish tomatoes, cucumbers and zucchini, the detritus of which will someday be tossed into the compost heap. It's an endless circle of life, and in the middle of that round cycle is the unspoken spoke, a dog who has designs on the middle of the earth, and is determined to overcome every obstacle to at last find the key to the puzzles we have set before her. We admire that in her.

Rubik's Dog! We got her. Come see for yourself.

CHAPTER
SIX

In the
Doghouse

But soon to be paroled.

Life is Good

by
Eve Gaal

I have seen many people wearing T-shirts that say *Life is Good*. When I do, I truly wonder about them and how they can disregard the pain and suffering in the world, throwing it figuratively under a magic carpet so they can live in their ostrich-like setup of make-believe happiness and good fortune. Men and women march off to war and some of them come back worse for wear. I think if I came back from battle, I'd probably want to punch the first guy I saw wearing one of those T-shirts. He'd at least need a few bandages.

My life, on the other hand, has been good. Very good. But our American Dream involved a lot of work. I married my own soldier and we bought our first house with a VA loan. We lived on a lovely hilltop an hour from a large metropolitan area, and creatively refigured our lives, our work and our future. Nothing was easy and nothing was handed to us on a silver platter.

In fact, life was somewhat hard, but rewarding. We had the standard dramas that included broken bones, an appendectomy, car problems and deaths in our family. As humble humans rescued by God, we prayed alongside strangers that were perfect parents with perfect children and our faith carried us onto tranquil pastures making our penance feel less severe. Of course that was *before* "Fiona."

Somewhere in the big book of destiny, we were chosen. In fact, it happened only a few weeks after my last confession. It was pretty standard—the confession, I mean. Maybe I left too much out or maybe I didn't say all my required Hail Mary's, but something went seriously askew regarding my reparations.

You see, shortly thereafter, we received a phone call that our daughter couldn't keep her 4-month-old Chihuahua and she had just brought it home from being spayed. She told us that her new apartment manager would not allow dogs and she didn't know what to do. What to do? Doesn't she know that the first dogs in line for the gas chamber are Chihuahuas? There are hundreds of them in our local shelters, pleading for adoption with accusing black beady eyes. "Of course," I said, "We'll take the helpless little dog."

A 4-month-old sounded so cute and cuddly, but when she brought Fiona over, it was clear that the dog didn't want to cuddle. She wanted to run around and investigate everything and mark things for her very own. The harnessed energy in this pup could send a man to the moon. Why should Californians depend on foreign oil when we have Chihuahuas? Maybe I should call the shelter and give them an idea. Who knows—nuclear energy today, and Mars tomorrow—all thanks to major doggy adrenaline.

Defying the speed of sound, her pointed ears are on the alert for every little noise and she appears to be communicating with extraterrestrials. Fast does not even begin to describe Fiona. Like an alien, she can beam herself ahead of me in the hall. Wait, I just left you sitting on the couch and here you are calmly standing by the door, staring up at me. How does this happen?

Who knew that puppy pads were for chewing and that Fiona preferred making her business inside air-conditioned comfort as opposed to a warm, shaded courtyard? The puppy poop that was a semi-unattractive novelty the first day now appeared in secret camouflaged places on my Persian rug.

We took her to the clinic for a checkup and she promptly peed all over the nurse. When we bought her a collar and a tag, she almost took my husband's hand off at the wrist. It took two Band-Aids. Her teeth are razor sharp and if she doesn't want to do something, she makes it very clear by clamping down hard and drawing blood. She's only 2 pounds, but we're running out of Band-Aids.

When our daughter calls and we complain about becoming Fiona's newest chew toys, she feels sorry for the dog. Thankfully, Fiona sleeps through the night, and though she's wearing out her welcome, things could always be worse. Just this morning my husband stepped into a hot, mushy pile next to our bed. At 4 months old, I don't expect her to be a genius, but why can't she come to us when we call her name? Should we change her name to Frita Bandita? Heck, then we'd be out eight bucks for the tag.

Currently, we have a love-hate relationship with the independent little bitch. Honestly, I think she's adorable and

I don't mind the extra mopping, cleaning, scrubbing and all around stinkiness. Time to make amends and repent my shortcomings, as in yes, I'm a sinner and I can't blame our little rescue for everything! Despite her wicked ways, things will improve and with God's help, life will once again be good for all of us. In the meantime, I'm buying Fiona a T-shirt that says *Life is Good*.

It's not the size of the dog in the fight,
it's the size of the fight in the dog.
~~ Mark Twain

Diamond in the Rough

by
Kathleene Baker

As an adult, "Maggie," our first black and silver Schnauzer was a jewel. She was obedient, loving and simply all anyone could hope for. However, as a youngster, she was a pup from hell with the curiosity of a cat! I so hoped she'd eventually mature and end her inquisitive ways before I had an all-out nervous breakdown.

By the time she was several months old, Mag had developed a fondness for standing on the bed with both front feet positioned on bedside tables. She sniffed, snooped and stretched as far as possible in search of anything entertaining. We did our best to keep tabletops clear of all items except the lamps. To head off any would-be disaster, we were always on the alert. Relaxing became a thing of the past.

One evening, I realized the little monster had abruptly vanished from sight and I sprinted to the bedroom. As I entered, gnawing sounds caught my attention. I found Maggie lazing upon my pillow, her fluffy, white beard sparkling in the lamplight. That beautiful beard was also swaying to and fro as she chewed relentlessly. I could only wonder, *What is it this time?* I reached into her mouth, pulled out her latest prize and gasped!

"Jerry, get in here!" I shouted to my husband.

Upon his arrival, I presented him with a mangled earring. It wasn't just any costume bobble—it was one of a new pair of diamond studs that Jerry had given me for Valentine's Day.

Thrilled that the earring had been retrieved and knowing bent prongs could be repaired, I glanced at the table to retrieve its mate. I struggled for breath . . . it was gone!

I peered under the bed skirt, under the table, ran my hands over the floral bedspread and then repeated my steps with a flashlight. After a 30-minute search, we concluded that the other earring had gone down the hatch and now rested in Maggie's tummy! Visions of the earring post perforating her stomach or intestine flashed through my mind, along with costly medical bills for surgery to save the little devil's life.

Knowing I'd never call unless it was urgent, our longtime vet had given us his home phone number years prior. I dialed with no hesitation that evening, ran the scenario by him, having to pause now and again while he snickered. I found nothing funny about the mess we were in and tried to ignore his weird sense of humor.

"Bob, what are we going to do? You need X-rays first thing in the morning, right?" I whimpered.

"No X-rays for now, Kathy! What you are going to do is pray for poop and sunshine!" His laughter was maniacal.

He explained that typically she would pass something the size of an earring, but I was to investigate each bowel movement for the next few days. Tongue depressors, dead twigs from shrubbery or an old pencil were suggested as tools. *Oh, joy, I can hardly wait.*

Nevertheless, it made sense—I could and would do it! Then I remembered his "sunshine" remark. In my frantic state of mind I had missed any connection whatsoever. Feeling foolish, I mumbled, "So, what's with the sunshine, Bob? What does that have to do with anything?"

With that, he flat-out roared! "If the sun is shining, the gold and diamond will as well, Kathy! It'll make your job so much easier." As much as we adored the man, I swear I would have kicked him had I been given the chance.

The following day, my eyes were never off Maggie, for fear she'd poop swiftly and I'd miss a movement. When darkness fell, I followed her with a flashlight, aimed precisely on her cute little butt. Day #1 was a complete failure.

The sun shone brightly on Day #2. Yet, with no success, I was getting mighty tired of digging for lost treasure. And by late afternoon, I was in a full-blown state of angst. I fed Maggie her last meal of the day, waited about 10 minutes, and then we headed outside. Knowing it was my last opportunity to "strike gold" until the following morning, I said a quick and selfish prayer . . . although I'm certain God doesn't listen to such nonsense.

Maggie did her deed. I arranged my usual layers of paper towels and placed the movement upon them, dead center, lest anything tumble into the deep, thick grass. With my first maneuver, gold glinted in the sunlight and I squealed! Continuing my investigation, I found the entire setting with post attached! It had, however, been chewed into a distorted wad. Next, the small, round back which slides up the post winked at me—it was in perfect condition. Whoo hoo! About to give up on more booty, I suddenly spied a slight dull glimmer. Yep—the diamond was right alongside the deformed clump of gold! All pieces had traveled in tandem on their dark passage back into a world filled with sunshine.

After an overnight soak with gobs of anti-bacterial Dawn, I rinsed over and over again with boiling water. All parts then went into a small jar of alcohol for a good shaking, swishing and an overnight soak.

Naturally, the jeweler did ask what had caused such extraordinary damage. I confessed it was Maggie, but omitted all details about my quest to recover lost treasure. I simply told him she was a rambunctious pup that we fondly called our little "Diamond in the Rough!"

My Amish Dog

by
Clara Wersterfer

Yep! You read the title right. I do believe "Onyx Two Toes"—my black Chihuahua with two white toes—is definitely Amish. I have many reasons for thinking this. Trust me, it is not my imagination!

For starters, she doesn't believe in taking medication of any kind, just like older generations within the Amish culture. Don't think you can fool her by hiding a pill in human food, as she'll shred it to bits before eating, always on the lookout for a pill, which she spits out. Onyx really doesn't like most people food anyway so she becomes quite suspicious whenever it's offered. She much prefers plain dry kibble. Just try to hide a pill there—it simply cannot be done.

Onyx doesn't like fancy clothes either, especially posh shoes. She has destroyed nine pairs of mine in a couple of months, but she won't touch the plain old work loafers, tennis shoes or even walking shoes.

My little dog does love to garden, just like the Amish. This is evidenced by all the plants she has pulled up. Once done with that chore, she'll then dig holes in various new locations for me to replant them. And, as a courtesy, she'll put the uprooted plants in a pile where she would like them to be relocated. Kind of her, isn't it? Then Onyx will help me with the watering, standing wherever the water's falling to ensure I am watering the proper place, barking furiously when she feels I should move the hose to another spot. Yes, she does get wet. However, she takes a bath on a daily basis for she loves to be clean. She also likes the towel drying, a good rubdown and a brisk brushing.

Another thing that seems Amish to me is the way Onyx loves to hear people singing. Belt out any old tune and she immediately joins in. She seems to favor gospel and bluegrass music, and always sings along when she hears a rousing hymn.

The final clue that Onyx is Amish is that she shuns me! Onyx does so whenever I have wronged to her. It's easy to do something she doesn't approve of, and when this occurs, I'm in big trouble.

During the process of shunning, Onyx ignores my pleas to come, turning her head a different direction and refusing to even look at me. I find myself begging for her forgiveness, but my words fall on deaf doggy ears. And during her uppity period of shunning, she insists on being carried outside for her potty breaks.

Onyx doesn't shun me for an hour or a day, but for four days minimum and sometimes as many as 10 days! My last 10-day penance was because I shook a single sheet of the newspaper at her. Believe me, I didn't strike her, I simply waved the paper. Straight away, Onyx headed to the bathroom and flopped down by the tub. Thinking she would pout a bit and get over it, I left her alone. But she didn't. Nightly, Onyx slept in the bathroom, instead of, as usual, in bed with me. Many times, I carried her to bed and she would go right back to the bathroom, sometimes getting into the tub to sleep.

After 10 days of dishing out the punishment she believed I deserved, Onyx decided to finally come to bed. However, not before she peered around the door for a couple of minutes, turning her head to the left and then to the right, but never looking directly at me. When she finally relented, she walked to my bed and asked to be lifted up. I had my precious, adorable, Amish baby back, at least until the next time I forget and wave a piece of paper to get her attention!

"The dearest things in life are mostly near at hand," is a fitting Amish proverb for the relationship Onyx and I share. Even though I am still learning the ways of this culture, I wouldn't trade my beloved Amish Chihuahua for all the non-Amish dogs in the world!

Choosing Her Chews

by
Terri Elders

From the day my husband, Ken, brought her home, the 7-week-old ball of curly-tailed Akita that we named "Tsunami," and called "Nami" for short, gnawed on everything. She chomped on the legs of the dining room chairs. She shredded the fringe on the rug in front of the fireplace in the den. She munched on reachable leaves of the potted ficus in the entryway. Her razor-sharp teeth even ripped a hole through my flannel blouse and grazed my arm when I lifted her away from the newly bedraggled plant.

Fortunately I glimpsed my scarlet Mongolian cashmere shawl as it floated down the hall and was lucky enough to snatch it from Nami's cavernous maw before she had a chance to convert it back into a skein of yarn.

"Oh, she's just a puppy . . . she'll outgrow it," Ken said, when I insisted that neither I nor my belongings really were intended to be chew toys.

I soon learned not to leave pencils atop my computer desk. Though still just a tiny pup, Nami already had figured out a way to leap onto my chair so she could paw them to the floor. Then she'd pounce on them and nibble them to splinters. She even swallowed their erasers.

Her appetite expanded to writing implements in general. I held up one to show Ken the remnants of what had once been a ballpoint pen. He merely shrugged.

"She's very bright," Ken said. "She comes from a long line of talented show dogs. She'll soon learn to leave our things alone."

Then one day Ken left some seasoned rib-eyes on the kitchen counter while he ducked outside to check if the briquettes were ready. When I heard him howl, I suspected Nami had treated herself to an early supper. I was right.

She had eaten only one of the steaks. When I asked if she'd devoured my steak or his, Ken sighed.

"She's very bright," I reminded him, "so it must have been yours. She wouldn't dare eat my dinner. I'm the one who takes her for walks."

We agreed we'd split the rib-eye and supplement our meal by tossing a couple of sausage links on the grill.

"It could have been worse," Ken said, with a rueful smile. "She could have eaten both the steaks."

"Yep," I agreed. "It's good that she was thoughtful enough to leave one for us."

Nami's need to gnaw didn't seem to be satisfied by traditional dog toys and treats. Sure, she'd play with her Kong until she could coax out the treat buried inside it. Otherwise, she preferred Ken's tennis shoes to her rawhide strips and my sunglasses to her tennis balls. One positive outcome was that our bedroom became much tidier as we learned not to leave any items on bedside tables or the floor.

Then one morning as I typed away at the computer, I heard a strange snarl from the den. I vaguely wondered what Nami had found to attack. I wrote a couple more sentences, then paused, curious about the clinks and snuffles from the next room.

I got up to explore. Our little dog lay splayed on the floor, intent on chewing on something pink. I could see twisted bits of metal and worried that it was something she could cut herself on. I reached down and wriggled the object from her mouth.

It was not a pretty sight. Apparently the night before, Ken had removed his partial dental plate and set it on the lamp table beside his recliner. Nami had found it, of course. The dentist's repair bill totaled nearly a thousand bucks. Ken didn't leave that plate unattended again.

Years later, we took Nami to visit Ken's son for New Year's weekend. We'd stayed up late New Year's Eve, sipping champagne and playing Hearts. The next morning, after a big breakfast of quesadillas, Ken flopped down on the sofa and announced he was taking a nap. My stepson, daughter-in-law and I moved to the dining room table to play Tripoley. Engrossed in the game, we didn't pay much attention to Nami.

After a while, I peered into the living room and found the dog chomping on something near the sofa where Ken still snoozed.

I've heard it said that lightning never strikes twice, that the same misfortune won't befall the same person more than once. I've also heard, "Once bitten, twice shy," which equates to the thought that if something goes wrong once then a person will be careful about doing the same thing again.

So much for those hoary old proverbs. I don't buy either one. After finishing his breakfast, Ken had absentmindedly placed his partial plate on the table lamp beside the sofa. And Nami found it!

Here's a pair of sayings I do believe: "There's just no accounting for taste" and "Truth is stranger than fiction." They also say a third time's a charm, but we were wise enough to never put that adage to the test.

Nami at 10 weeks

The Dog Whisperer Shakes His Head

by

Gregory Lamping

"You need to be the boss!"

Those are the words I keep hearing from Cesar Millan, the self-proclaimed "Dog Whisperer." As a dog owner, I know I should be the boss, the pack leader, the alpha male, but there are some dogs that adamantly refuse to get with the program.

Take "Monkey," my Border Collie. He's too quirky and stubbornly independent to go along with who's the boss and who's following whom and all that stuff.

Most dogs, for instance, love a car ride. They would leap through flaming hoops over a pit of hungry crocodiles to get into a car. Not Monkey.

I decided to drive him to the park for a walk today. Opening the car door, I told him to get in. He looked up at me as if to say, "Why?" I felt like telling him, "Well, we can either just stand here and grow old together and let our neighbors peek out their windows every now and then wondering why we're still standing in the driveway looking like idiots, or YOU CAN GET IN THE CAR!!!"

Since he's not one for sensible explanations, I tossed a doggy treat onto the back seat. He looked it over, thinking, "Hmm, I wonder if that's one of those cheap doggy biscuits made out of the same flour marked 'famine relief,' or does it contain some real meat?" He concluded it was probably made from famine-relief flour and not worth a jump.

I then opened the opposite car door and peered at him from the other side, vigorously clapping my hands, saying, "Come on, Monkey! Hop in! You can do it!" He ignored my cheers. I went to Plan D, pleading, "Monkey, please. Be a good boy. Get into the car. Pleee-ee-eease!" And when that didn't work, I launched Plan E: I lifted him into the car, pushed his butt forward with both hands, and slammed the door.

I imagined the Dog Whisperer telling me, "You need to be a calm and assertive leader and show confidence!" I know, but my way is better than growing old together, standing in the driveway and waiting for the confidence to kick in.

When we got to the park, Monkey decided he wanted to stay in the car. The dog that didn't want to get in the car in the first place now refused to get out! He closed his eyes to nap, but I had no patience for this game. I clipped the leash to his collar and pulled him out of the backseat.

Later in the walk, I let Monkey off leash so he could break free and run circles around me, pretending I'm a little lost lamb in need of some direction. On our way back to the car, however, I noticed he was falling farther and farther behind, like a teenage boy too embarrassed to be seen walking with his parents to a church sing-along.

By the time I got to the parking lot, he was so far behind I wasn't sure he was even following me at all. In the distance, I spotted him lying under a tree, nonchalantly enjoying the weather, not realizing that trying to survive in the park for the rest of his life without me could easily turn into his worst nightmare.

Since I know he wouldn't hear me if I called him—even if I used a blow horn—I went back to where he was lying. Once he saw that I was about to clip the leash on him, he jumped up and playfully attacked it. I then walked back to the car, pulling Monkey with his jaws clamped on the leash, telling him, "Wowee, you are one tough guy! What big muscles!"

And to that, I envisioned the Dog Whisperer turning away and shaking his head.

My Fowl Little Puppy

by
Linda O'Connell

What do you call a feathered canine? I called mine "Dusty." She and her 8-week-old littermates—part Springer Spaniel and who-knows-what-else—were on display in a large metal crate behind a viewing window at a local department store. They sold everything under the sun, including puppies for $7 each.

As her four littermates nestled in their large floor-level crate, I watched her chomp at the latch and cautiously make her great escape. I thought the little brown pup was injured when I saw her right forepaw and leg. It was completely white—she looked like she had a cast on. Even if she had been wearing a cast, nothing could have stopped her. I snickered as she tore into a bag of kibble and ate until she had a puffer-fish belly. Then she ran back and forth, in and out of her cage, yapping and tugging on her littermates until they were all free-roaming mutts. She was a little rambunctious. Those puppies ate and pooped to their heart's content.

The scrawny kid in charge of the pet department returned from his break. He entered the glass enclosure and stepped over piddles and piles. The look of disapproval on his face made my heart sink. I tapped on the window and pointed to the troublemaker. He nodded with a disgusted look and mouthed, "I know!" And I knew too, right then and there.

I was a 19-year-old newlywed, and my 20-year-old husband walked up just as the clerk placed the puppy in my arms. "This is our baby," I said, as proud as any new mother.

We couldn't think of a name for her. I vetoed Killer and Butch, and he groaned at Daisy and Brownie. We went to the drive-in movie that Friday evening, and when a little boy saw her in my arms at the concession stand, he asked, "Is that Dusty's dog?" That little kid had no idea that he had just named our baby.

I put a ticking clock in Dusty's cardboard-box bed and waited till she was snoozing. It was still difficult to leave her and go to work Monday. I reasoned that she had an empty apartment to roam and a buffet at her disposal. She paper trained so quickly that in two days, she was doing her "doodie" in the right place. When I came home, I wrapped her foul mess in newspaper and praised my baby. Then I noticed her rawhide bones and squeaky toys on the floor in the same place they had been that morning. "What did you play with all day?" I baby talked to her as I took her outdoors.

It wasn't until I walked back in that I noticed her new play toys. The chair legs looked like a beaver had been by for a bite while we were gone. My favorite pair of shoes was minus the straps and one had a peek-a-boo toe. Ahh!

Scolding her worked—she crawled under the bed. Then she slowly nosed her way out. She was so darned cute, I had to scoop her up and instantly forgive her. I grabbed a brown crayon and rubbed the color right back into the chair legs before my husband arrived home. I crayoned the legs on the kitchen chair, an end table and the dresser. I tossed my favorite shoes.

Dusty and I grew up together; she helped me survive the overwhelming loneliness and misery I experienced when my husband was drafted and sent thousands of miles away. She was a wonderful companion, with a receptive vocabulary that was astonishing. Every dog worth his kibble responds to the question, "Go bye-bye?" Dusty seemed to understand everything I said. On command she would get the correct one of her five squeaky toys albeit without their squeakers, because she chewed every single one of them silent. I could reprimand her in my normal speaking voice and she would scoot under the bed or behind the couch, depending upon which room we were in.

She had the silkiest, wavy coat, and many nights I used her fur to sop up my tears. For some reason, as smart as her mind was, her body was confused. She grew a thick, wavy coat every spring and continued to fluff up all through the summer, and then, as the first leaves of autumn fell, she began to shed along with the trees. Her fur was sparse and she didn't stay outdoors for very long in the winter. The rest of the year she heard the call of the wild and enjoyed chasing squirrels in the park, swimming in the creek or romping in the yard.

She grew into a medium-sized dog and she outgrew her nasty chewing habit, but that didn't mean she behaved herself. One day, I came home from work and as I headed upstairs, I thought I saw a giant chicken dart by. Feathers were flying in every direction. I almost turned and ran back out the door. Then I realized the little dickens was up to her old tricks. I took the steps two at a time and stopped in my tracks. Feathers were floating in the air, covering the floor and trailing from one room to the other. I sat down and waited patiently for Dusty to come out. Oh, yeah, she knew she was in trouble! When she thought the coast was clear, she bounded into the room, head down and rolled through the contents of our bed pillows. She slipped and slid. Covered in feathers from head to tail, she looked at me as I looked at her. I had to get even with her.

Finally, that day came for my dear Dusty a few years later. We had had a daughter and she loved to dress Dusty like the sibling she thought she was. I captured the moments on 8MM, with movies of Dusty wagging her tail, strutting along with my 3-year-old as though they were trotting down the runway, wearing the latest feathered and ruffled fashions. I'm not too sure she was overly embarrassed, but I felt vindicated, nonetheless.

Dusty gave me unconditional love and 15 years' worth of pleasure, pain, happiness, heartache, laughter and tears. Whether the fur is shedding or the feathers are flying, what is a relationship with a beloved dog but a seesaw ride of ups and downs?

I Love Lucy

by

Linda Lohman

I have a roommate. She weighs 10 pounds, has four feet and answers to the name of "Lucy." A full-bred Yorkie, Lucy was previously a breeder. But her tendency to tell other mothers how to behave like ladies made her quite unpopular. So unpopular, in fact, that one of them took a bite out of her left eye. That disfigurement left her jobless. Since she didn't qualify for unemployment, she became adoptable.

Some people might say she is spoiled. I say she is a pampered princess with definite duties. She takes her chores seriously. Her favorite is to tell me it is time for bed at night. However she has a full day of doggy tasks.

Yorkie jobs are not unlike other dog chores. Her first mission in the morning is to dance. She is so excited to greet me coming out of the bathroom that her pirouettes are worthy of the Russian ballet. She was probably a ballerina in a previous life.

Her second chore is to take me for a walk. Most people walk their dogs, but Lucy has a mind of her own. She walks me. She would like to run me, but for my arthritic knees, walking and running are exactly the same. We walk/run for about 40 minutes. Sometimes she forgets that I am on the other end of the leash as she pulls me toward a prized squirrel or the neighborhood wild turkey.

Lucy is especially adept at making it to her imaginary finish line if there is another dog already there. With her 12-foot leash, she attempts to pull and jerk my arm out of socket. We are thinking of entering a tractor-pulling contest. Is there a Yorkie division?

Although Lucy cannot sing one note of *Shall We Gather at the River*, she remains a loyal Baptist. Somewhere she must have tithed because she leaves regular contributions at the Baptist church. When her back is turned, I dispose of them.

After our marathon hike, Lucy is so hungry for breakfast that she will accept food in any form. This is my chance to score any pills she might need—I slip them into a tasty morsel.

Her afternoon duty is to watch the doors and windows. Since I am hearing-impaired, she will alert me if any ominous bird, butterfly or squirrel comes within 100 feet of our yard. Should the doorbell ring, she has a separate and distinct bark to let me know that this is BUSINESS!

Lucy alternates barking and napping chores until noon, when an internal alarm says it is time to prance to the corner. She needs to check out blades of grass and pretends to find just the right one. All the while she is doing squirrel reconnaissance.

At precisely 6 P.M., Lucy's internal alarm shatters any sound barrier. Her evening walk/run takes a different route. Our evening poop-loop, walk/run encounters an abundance of dogs, all of them pulling leashes with their owners attached.

Lucy has a running feud with two white Poodles that jog across the street. In her Rottweiler voice, she tells them to stay on their side of the street. I know she says this because they pretend not to understand her.

And I know her Doberman voice from her German Shepherd growl. Rottweiler is used when she gets mean, and Lucy's 10 pounds of mean is a quivering mass. She becomes a Yorkie terror!

A Westie named "Cloud" is her friend. They exchange backside sniffs and go their own way. Most other dogs warrant only a cursory sniff, as if she is saying, "I have business to take care of."

Another Yorkie—"Buster"—is her favorite sniffer. She smiles as she pulls the leash toward him, much like lovers running to each other in fields of clover. They enjoy getting their leashes tangled and their yips and yaps convey the message, "OK, it's your turn to sniff." She flirts visibly with Buster, making many seductive twists to look over her shoulder at him. This is the verbal equivalent of a woman licking her lips and touching her hair. I swear I've seen her wink at him with her blind eye.

Once we are back to the pull of the leash, Lucy again is transformed into the equivalent of an entire sled dog team. And herein lies the problem. For all of her leading, driving, pulling and tugging—Lucy does not have a license!

Linda and Lucy

Doggy Revenge

by

Valerie Benko

They say revenge is sweet. Here's what I've always wondered: who is "they" and how "sweet" was the revenge? And does it extend to the animal kingdom?

The first time I met the gray puppy with the floppy ears, pink nose and beautiful baby blues, he tried to bite my face. In fact, that was how my next several visits with him went. My sister cradled her little Weimaraner named "Rouger" and gently scolded him. He was her sweet baby. I thought he was Cujo.

As the months passed, the attempts at face-biting were reduced to hand-nibbling and our relationship began to build. He was a playful and active puppy, quickly growing into a dog who welcomed me with a voracious wag of the tail and a wet tongue. We were finally on the good track.

When my sister, Ginger, asked me to dog-sit over the 4th of July holiday, I readily accepted. I would spend the night on the

3rd and then drive Rouger to her mother-in-law's house on the 4th.

I don't think I had ever had a dog in my car before. What could possibly go wrong? But I was worried he might distract me. Fortunately, my brother-in-law had an answer to the solution—a shock collar. Rouger was being trained to hunt birds and the collar prevented him from running off and not coming back. He suggested that maybe Rouger would behave better in the car with it on.

I did as my brother-in-law instructed, slipping the electronic collar on Rouger for our car ride. But I didn't turn it on, as I had no intention of using it. My hope was that he would respect the collar and behave.

A few miles from my sister's house, I crashed into a truck that failed to complete a stop at the intersection. During the collision, Rouger slammed into the back of my seat, breaking my neck. I knew I was OK. I couldn't turn my head, but I could move my legs. As the ambulance drove me away, all I could think about was how scared poor Rouger must be and how dumb I was to put the shock collar on him. He probably thought he was a bad dog when he wasn't.

I was in the hospital for a few days and on one of my sister's visits, she announced that Rouger had destroyed my purse and wallet. I didn't care. I figured I deserved it after the stress and anxiety I'd put him though. Although he and I didn't have any problems after that, I do think he held a grudge. And on a cold November day, I was about to find out.

Lazy snowflakes swirled in the wind and drifted to the frozen earth. I peered out of the kitchen window to gauge travel conditions. Even with flurries, it was warmer than usual on Thanksgiving Day in Pennsylvania and the roads were bare. It would be a good day to travel to my sister's house for a turkey dinner with the family.

I was on dessert duty and I grabbed my homemade pumpkin cheesecake out of the refrigerator. My husband and I packed our car and started on our 40-minute journey to my sister's house with thoughts of delicious food dancing through our heads—his favorite being a savory oyster stuffing, and mine, my sister's wonderful hot dinner rolls, dripping with butter. To me, no Thanksgiving Day meal is truly complete without a hot buttery roll.

When we arrived, the windows were fogged up from the warmth of the house meeting the cold air outside. The turkey was being cut and its juicy aroma pulled me toward the kitchen which was alive with the clatter of dishes and voices.

I said my greetings and found a home for the pumpkin cheesecake. Ginger immediately put me on drink duty and then casually added that there would not be any rolls for dinner.

Her words were like a record player scratching to a stop. *No rolls? Did she forget? Did she not have time?* I thought, trying to get over the shock. In that moment, all I could envision was missing out on a blob of butter melting on a hot roll.

"Rouger ate them. All of them," she continued, with a hint of anger lacing her words.

I shouldn't have been surprised, but I was. It turned out that while everyone was out of the kitchen, Rouger pulled down both pans and graciously helped himself to 24 dinner rolls! My sister went looking for the rolls to put them in the bread basket and was confused when they were nowhere to be found. As she discovered two empty pans lying under the dining room table, confusion turned to clarity and then to anger when she realized who the guilty party was.

After dinner, I was perusing Black Friday ads on her couch when Rouger walked into the room. Our eyes met and he held my gaze. I shook my head. He had finally gotten his revenge.

Ginger and Rouger

Yoga Puppy

by
John Schlimm

The first time I did yoga, I unrolled by moss-green mat on the living room floor in front of the television and popped in my new *OM YOGA* DVD.

"Let's begin our sun salutations by standing in *tadasana*, mountain pose," the yoga instructor, Cyndi Lee, began.

I stood straight, feeling my leg bones reach down as my leg muscles stretched up. "Yoga is always moving in two directions," Cyndi explained.

That's when I heard the jingling of dog tags approaching.

While working on separating my toes so I'd have "nice, big, juicy wide feet," as Cyndi called them, my dog, "Little Coyote," raced into the room. Rescued months earlier by some kids who found him under an abandoned car, Little Coyote was bald, shivering, and nearly starved to death. Now he was a healthy, medium-sized puff of wild and mischievous white fur.

With wide eyes and a panting tongue, my friend lapped around me, breaking my beginner's concentration, and finally stopped behind me in the middle of my mat.

"You can't stay there," I told him. Little Coyote came to live with us following a brief stint at the Humane Society. It was love at first sight, though I wasn't feeling too fond of him just then as he invaded my narrow green mat.

His response to my admonition was to stretch his front paws out in front of him, curving his upper back downward while reaching his chin upward. He then sat down.

"Little Coyote, you have to move!" I became frustrated, afraid I'd miss out on the blissful endpoint of my yoga session if I didn't have complete silence and concentration.

"Let's inhale the arms out and up," my TV yoga master beckoned. "As you exhale, fold over the legs."

I did as I was told by the yoga master, hoping Little Coyote would get the message and move off my mat. But, no, he was determined to stake his claim on the same 2x6 foot space I was occupying. I even nudged him with my right foot, but he wouldn't budge. Now I was showing aggression, a big no-no for an aspiring yogi.

Soon, Cyndi snapped me back, saying, "Inhale . . . step the right leg back into a long lunge." Little Coyote wasn't moving, so I swung my right leg up and over him.

Then it was time for my left leg to go, up and over the dog.

Suddenly, I found myself in the same pose I had just seen Little Coyote perform, which I then realized is called "downward facing dog" for a reason. Only, my downward dog pose all too literally entailed looking down face-to-face, at a ball of fur grinning up at me with his tongue hanging out.

Later, while I was heaving both feet up and over him again, a recycling truck stopped in front of my house. The driver started to dump glass bottles, making a ruckus, which sent Little Coyote into a barking fit. The distraction caused me, in midair, to twist to the side and crash to the floor.

"Be quiet!" I yelled, rising and stomping back onto my mat. Now I was angry, another yoga no-no.

The recycling truck gone, Little Coyote reassumed his calm. For the next several minutes, Cyndi had me twisting this way and stretching arms that way, balancing one elongated leg behind me while bending the other. All the while, Little Coyote watched from beneath me, licking my ankles.

"And this time, let your toes shift you forward and come into an upward dog," Cyndi instructed.

There was no way to do this without squishing Little Coyote, which was tempting at the moment. Instead, I finally pushed him off the mat. Now I felt guilty, which completely defeated the purpose of releasing tension.

Little Coyote raced around me, taunting me. He then did his own upward facing dog, as if saying, "Look what I can do better than you." I do admit, Cyndi would have marveled at his precision. When my yoga session ended, I didn't feel enlightened or calm whatsoever. Little Coyote, however, strolled out of the living room, the picture of peace.

Two days later, I again unrolled my moss-green mat and popped Cyndi Lee into the DVD player. And again, before I struck mountain pose, I heard the jingling of dog tags growing closer. I was soon matching Little Coyote, downward facing dog for downward facing dog, once again.

However, it was while I was in tree pose this time—with Little Coyote biting my big toe, causing me to teeter—that a breakthrough revelation struck me. Maybe I was wrong here, growing frustrated and angry? Maybe Little Coyote, who had endured suffering in the cruelest way under that old car, was trying to teach me something right then and there? Maybe his dalliances on my mat were, in reality, the natural eloquence that embodies the very meaning of yoga? Maybe I had two teachers in the room with me, one on television and the other in living, breathing, furry flesh? While the first teacher imparted the technicalities of centuries-old poses and breathing, my second teacher taught me the essence of the practice, how to pause, to lighten-up, to relax, to embrace and release the life around me.

After that revelation, the moss green mat quickly became OUR magic carpet. After that when I heard his jingling tags approaching—I'd invite Little Coyote into the ebb and flow of my yoga practice. I would gently nudge him to the side when doing upward facing dog (so I didn't squish him), but I also watched in admiration as he performed his own flawless downward facing dog. And, when Cyndi Lee concluded with "*Namaste!*" followed by a bow, I turned to Little Coyote and, with a smile and a bow, I thanked him.

"*Namaste*, Yoga Puppy!"

NYMB Series Founders

Together, Dahlynn and Ken McKowen have 60-plus years of professional writing, editing, publication, marketing and public relations experience. Full-time authors and travel writers, the two have such a large body of freelance work that when they reached more than 2,000 articles, stories and photographs published, they stopped counting. And the McKowens are well respected ghostwriters, having worked with CEOs and founders of some of the nation's biggest companies. They have even ghostwritten for a former U.S. president and a few California governors and elected officials.

From 1999 to 2009, Ken and Dahlynn were consultants and coauthors for *Chicken Soup for the Soul*, where they collaborated with series founders Jack Canfield and Mark Victor Hansen on several books such as *Chicken Soup for the Entrepreneur's Soul; Chicken Soup for the Soul in Menopause; Chicken Soup for the Fisherman's Soul;* and *Chicken Soup for the Soul: Celebrating Brothers and Sisters*. They also edited and ghost-created many more *Chicken* titles during their tenure, with Dahlynn reading more than 100,000 story submissions.

For highly acclaimed outdoor publisher Wilderness Press, the McKowen's books include national award-winner *Best of California's Missions, Mansions and Museums; Best of Oregon and Washington's Mansions, Museums and More;* and *The Wine-Oh! Guide to California's Sierra Foothills.*

Under Publishing Syndicate, the couple authored and published *Wine Wherever: In California's Mid-Coast & Inland Region*, and are actively researching wineries for *Wine Wherever: In California's Paso Robles Region*, the second book in the Wine Wherever series.

If that's not enough, the McKowens are also the creators of the Wine Wherever iPhone mobile winery-destination journaling app and are currently creating a travel television show under the same brand (www.WineWherever.com).

Shilo and Coco

About Kathleene S. Baker

Hi, Hank Baker here.

As the oldest fur boy in our home, I will speak on behalf of my little sisters Samantha and Abby, even though they both pitched Texas hissy fits when they found out I was the one writing this bio!

Mom is the only daughter of Lovey and Raymond Boucher. She grew up as a country girl outside of Augusta, Kansas. We fur kids are very confused, because Mom has two older brothers. I'm gonna ask our grandpa for an explanation because everyone knows brothers and sisters are born at the same time. Strange, huh?

After high school Mom graduated from Wichita Business College and had some great jobs she loved. Then she raised kids and fur kids.

We are so proud of our mom. When she told us she was creating a book on dogs, we yapped like crazy and helped her celebrate. She promised if we were very patient, when the book was done we'd get new toys and we'd have a party. *Woof, woof!*

While creating this book, Mom read all the fun stories to us and we helped her pick out the most perfect ones. Who would know a good dog story better than us dogs? Wow, some of those dogs were naughtier than any of us. Mom laughed and laughed, but I don't think she'd have laughed like that if we pulled some of those same stunts. Anyway, without us, she might have created a flop!

Sometimes we interrupted her work. You know, begging to go outside even if we didn't need to. Smart, aren't we? Or, we'd slap her arm when she was tapping on that typing machine. Usually a mouse would fall and bonk one of us right on our head. It worked though—she'd kiss us, love on us and forget about work for a while.

Dad helped too, which made Mom really happy. He learned how to do all kinds of new chores around the house. Once he said, "I never thought I'd finally retire, only to have my wife spend more time with a computer than with me." He brags about her and this wonderful book all of the time.

Biographer Hank seated on the floor with Mom,
with Abby and Samantha on the ottomon

Contributor Bios

Diana Amadeo is a multi-award-winning author with over 500 pieces published in books, e-books, magazines, and newspapers and online. Visit her web page at http://home.comcast.net/da.author/site/

Janice Arenofsky is a nationally published writer whose articles have appeared in such venues as *Newsweek, Scientific American, Experience Life* and *Healthy Pet.* For more information: www.janicearenofsky.com.

Francine Baldwin-Billingslea is mother and grandmother, a second-time-around newlywed and a breast-cancer survivor who has recently found a passion for writing. She has been published in over 20 anthologies, several magazines and authored her inspirational memoir titled *Through It All and Out on the Other Side* in the last five years.

Valerie Benko is a communications specialist and author from western Pennsylvania. She graduated from Slippery Rock University in 2002 with a bachelor's degree in communications. Valerie had been published in multiple anthologies and online. To see a complete list of her writing credits, visit http://valeriebenko.weebly.com.

Dennis C. Bentley is an IT consultant in St. Louis and resides in Hillsboro, Missouri. He is a part-time blogger, food critic, grave finder and member of the Writers Society of Jefferson County. Publications: *My Father is My Hero, My Teacher is My Hero* and *My Dog is My Hero.* www.dcbentley.com

Ireta Black will turn 90 years old in January, 2013. This story marks her second published work in less than a year. She is the aunt of Ken and Dahlynn McKowen and loves their many visits, especially when they all go out for animal-styled burgers at In-N-Out!

Carol Brosowske is a native Texan and resides in Plano, Texas, with husband Jim. Carol writes a weekly column for *FrankTalk* magazine, has three grown children, three dogs and would love to have more dogs—not children. Her many and varied hobbies include writing, quilting and cross-stitch.

Sallie Wagner Brown used to be a race car driver and a teacher; now she is a boater, a traveler and a writer. She, her husband and three dogs live on Hood Canal in Northwest Washington state where her surroundings both inspire her and make it difficult to concentrate.

Kathe Campbell lives on a Montana mountain with her donkeys, kitties and a Keeshond. Three children, 11 grands and three greats round out her herd. She is a prolific writer on Alzheimer's and contributing author to the *Chicken Soup for the Soul* series, *RX for Writers*, magazines and medical journals.

Barbara Carpenter is an award-winning author and poet with three novels and two memoirs in print. Her works appear in national magazines, anthologies and online publications. A co-creator of two *NYMB* titles—*On Special Occasions* and *On Dieting*—Barbara is also working on four new novels.

Elynne Chaplik-Aleskow is a Pushcart Prize nominated author and award-winning educator and broadcaster. She is founding general manager of WYCC-TV/PBS and distinguished professor emeritus of Wright College in Chicago. Her stories and essays have been published in numerous anthologies and magazines. Her husband Richard is her muse. Visit http://LookAroundMe.blogspot.com.

Carol Clouse is an architect, artist and author of the recently published inspirational memoir, *Clouse's Houses—A Story of Challenge, Creativity and the Heart of an Architect.* Carol divides residency between Montana and her home state of Pennsylvania, where she is working toward her master's degree in architecture.

Mark Crider, a native Texan, resides in Corpus Christi, Texas, with wife, Sandra, and Latte, his spoiled fur kid. He's an avid animal activist and devotes his time 24/7 working with rescue groups across the entire country through his organization Rescues Across America (RAA). It is his passion and life's calling.

Jerry Davis, DVM, a retired USAF colonel, and his wife of 46 years reside on a farm near his boyhood home. With a doctorate in veterinary medicine, his primary position was the care of German Shepherds used for service in the Vietnam War. He also holds a master's degree in public health.

Terri Elders lives near Colville, Washington, with two dogs (Tsunami and Natty) and three cats (Groucho, Harpo and Chico). A lifelong writer and editor, her stories have appeared in dozens of periodicals and anthologies. She blogs at atouchoftarragon. blogspot.com. Terri is a public member of the Washington state Medical Quality Assurance Commission.

Joanne Faries lives in Texas with her husband Ray. She's published in *Doorknobs & Bodypaint* and *Silver Boomer* anthologies. Joanne is a film critic for the *Little Paper of San Saba*. Look for her humorous memoir, *My Zoo World: If All Dogs Go to Heaven, Then I'm in Trouble*. http://wordsplash-joannefaries.blogspot.com

Marnie Frances became influenced to write by authors Richie Tankersley Cusick and Becca Fitzpatrick. She lives in Staffordshire, England with her two dogs.

Patricia Frank is co-owner of *FrankTalk* publication in Michigan, a lifelong animal advocate and writes a weekly column in their publication *Critter Corner*. She is involved in rescue and volunteerism to benefit animals of all species. Attempting to educate humans, Patricia lends a passionate voice for all earthly creatures that have none.

Eve Gaal's writing has appeared in various anthologies such as *Fiction Noir: Thirteen Stories, God Makes Lemonade, My Funny Valentine* and *Goose River* anthology. All are available on Amazon. Find more of Eve's writing at http://thedesertrocks.blogspot.com.

Joanne Gardner, husband Jack, and their houseful of animals reside in Tom Bean, Texas. Joanne taught school for many years and worked for an animal clinic until retirement. She has many interests including reading, her fur kids and time spent with her kids and grandkids. Painting is her true passion.

Betty Guenette has written numerous award-winning short stories and been published on-line and in magazines, newspapers and anthologies. She is currently compiling her diary of Thalia's escapades into a novella format. Betty is a member of the Sudbury Writers' Guild and Canadian Authors Association.

Renee Hughes is a CPA with an MBA, employed in communications privacy in St. Louis, Missouri. She is married with two adult children. Interests include writing, reading, acoustic guitar, church activities and collecting quotes and indie/alternative music. Pet: rescued rabbit. www.squirrelb8.com

Betty Keel has taught English grammar/literature for 33 years at colleges and universities throughout the United States, Europe and Asia. Betty and her husband enjoy their rustic farm house in the Georgia woodlands. They publish a travel magazine, care for stray and domestic animals and thank God for their many blessings.

Rebecca Kragnes is a pianist and composer living in Minneapolis, Minnesota, with her husband and their Seeing Eye Dogs®. Visit her website at http://rebeccak.com.

Gregory Lamping is a psychiatric nurse living in Kirkwood, Missouri. He enjoys daily hikes with his darling beagle, Scooter, and his Border collie, Monkey, who no longer has any problems getting in and out of cars.

Jaye Lewis is an award-winning inspirational author who celebrates life from the unique perspective of seeing miracles in the day-to-day. Jaye lives and writes in the Blue Ridge Mountains of Virginia. She shares her home with her family, four dogs and three cats. Visit www.entertainingangels.org or her blog at www.entertainingangelsencouragingwords.blogspot.com.

Linda Lohman is a *NYMB* first-time contributor. She thanks her parole officer, Lucy, the four-footed Yorkie that encourages daily use of the exercise yard. Living in Sacramento, California, she is retired and loving life. She's previously been published in six *Chicken Soup for the Soul* books. You may reach her at laborelations@yahoo.com.

Rolland Love is a bestselling and award-winning author and actor of film and stage. He presents workshops about Lewis and Clark and why it's important to write your life story. He has also published computer books, fiction novels, short stories and co-authored a cookbook with Ozark Mountains recipes. www.ozarkstories.com

Glady Martin lives in a small hamlet in British Columbia, Canada, where she enjoys sharing her stories through words. Having written since grade school, she says, "Writing is a way of breathing for me . . . it is a wonderful tool for expressing myself." Glady also enjoys writing poetry. Email: gladymartin1@shaw.ca

Gina Mulligan has written articles for national magazines such as *Ladies' Home Journal, Home and Garden, AAA* and *PC Computing*. She is the founder of Girls Love Mail, a charity that collects handwritten letters of encouragement and distributes them to women going through breast cancer treatment.

Pat Nelson, writer and editor, is co-creator of three upcoming *NYMB* books: *On Parenting, On Grandparenting* and *Working for a Living*. She has written newspaper columns, contributed to *Chicken Soup for the Soul*, written the book, *You...The Credit Union Member* and is currently writing a nonfiction book about a tuberculosis sanatorium.

Linda O'Connell, a preschool teacher from St. Louis, Missouri, is an award-winning inspirational and humor writer. Her husband, children and grandchildren fill her life with happiness and her heart with love. Linda blogs at www.http//lindaoconnell.blogspot.com.

Nelson O. Ottenhausen, a retired Army officer living in Gulf Breeze, Florida, has six published novels, a book of poetry entitled *Flowers, Love & Other Things*, and a short story featured in *Chicken Soup for the Fisherman's Soul*.

James Pearson, a native Texan, resides in Colorado Springs, Colorado, with wife, Serena, and two service dogs—Hero and Callaway. Jim enjoys writing, reading and could not live without a dog/dogs, service dogs or otherwise. El Pomar, his first service dog, provided confidence, security and was also Jim's utmost confidant.

Kathy Pippig lives in California with her husband and furry family. She has written six novels. Her award-winning poetry and short stories have been featured in newspapers, magazines and online publications. Kathy writes to reach the reader's heart and mind and make a difference.

Marsha Porter has co-authored a movie review guide, had a monthly column and published over 200 articles. Currently, she teaches high school English and dreams of penning the next great American novel.

Becky Povich discovered she was a writer in 2001, at the extreme young age of 48 years old. She writes personal essays and is about to complete her memoir *From Pig Tails to Chin Hairs: A Memoir & More*. Becky blogs at www.BeckyPovich.blogspot.com and can be reached at writergal53@gmail.com.

Frank Ramirez is a writer, pastor and a dog lover. He and his wife, Jennie, share three children, three grandchildren and two dogs—Toby the Collie, who visits nursing homes, and Duncan the rescue Collie mix, who means well. They live in the Snake Spring Valley in Pennsylvania.

Cappy Hall Rearick is a syndicated newspaper humor columnist, award-winning short story writer and novelist. Featured by the Erma Bombeck Writers Workshop as a humor writer of the month, Rearick's columns and short fiction can be read and enjoyed throughout the country in newspapers, anthologies and online.

John Reas is a former U.S. Army officer and telecommunications project manager. He resides in Plano, Texas, with two wonderful daughters, his wife's mother and his ever-so-patient wife. She allows John to dabble in his countless hobbies, of which writing has become his new passion.

Sioux Roslawski rescues dogs for "Love a Golden Retriever," a St. Louis-based rescue group. She has "failed" as a foster mom for LAGR and could not give up Foley…she and her husband *had* to adopt him. Sioux can be reached at http://siouxspage.blogspot.com.

Maggie Ryland, DVM, is a semi-retired veterinarian who lives with her husband, two dogs and three cats in a rural part of Stevens County in northeast Washington state. She does volunteer work with the Colville Valley Animal Sanctuary and has never yet been asked to treat a cougar.

John Schlimm is the international award-winning author of such books as *Grilling Vegan Style, The Tipsy Vegan, Twang: A Novel,* and *The Ultimate Beer Lover's Cookbook.* Also an activist, artist and educator, he holds a master's degree in education from Harvard University. For more information, please visit www.John-Schlimm.com.

Maggie Lamond Simone is a national award-winning columnist. Her books include *From Beer to Maturity* and POSTED! Her essays are featured in *P.S. What I Didn't Say,* multiple *Chicken Soup for the Soul* editions and *Cosmopolitan.* She is a professor of journalism and public speaking and also blogs for *The Huffington Post.*

Bobby Barbara Smith is known widely for her short stories and poetry published in *Memories & Motherhood* and *Faith Writers Speak,* as well as online. She enjoys gardening, singing and performing with various musicians. Bobby currently resides in north central Arkansas with her husband and two fur babies. Email: indy113@yahoo.com

Terri Tiffany counseled adults, owned a Christian bookstore and now resides in Texas with her husband. Her work has appeared in magazines, Sunday school take-home papers, and anthologies such as *Chicken Soup for the Soul* and *Blue Mountain Arts.* Please visit her at http://terri-treasures.blogspot.com.

Pat Wahler is a freelance writer from Missouri, where she resides with her husband, dog and cat. Her work has been published in dozens of local and national venues. A life-long animal lover, Pat ponders critters, writing and life's little mysteries at www.critteralley.blogspot.com.

Angela Walker currently resides in Liberty, Texas, with three Collies (Chloe, Runner and Wilson Henry) and a Sheltie by the name of Trevor Wayne. She has been a volunteer with Houston Collie Rescue for approximately 8 years and always has one foster. Angela has had several stories published in *Petwarmers.*

Clara Wersterfer resides in New Braunfels, Texas, with numerous fur kids. She has enjoyed a lifelong love affair with animals, whether they have fur, feathers or fins. Clara enjoys entertaining friends with tales of her babies. She has been published in *Petwarmers* and *Heartwarmers* newsletters and other Internet e-zines.

Kathy Whirity is a syndicated newspaper columnist who shares her sentimental musings on family life. She and her husband, Bill, share their home with Hannah and Henry, their regal retrievers in residence. Visit Kathy's website: www.KathyWhirity.com.

Story Permissions

Cheers, Teddy! © 2009 Diana M. Amadeo
Lost and Found © 2012 Janice Arenofsky
Diamond in the Rough © 2012 Kathleene S. Baker
Story of the Homestead © 21012 Kathleene S. Baker
Because of Max © 2012 Francine L. Baldwin-Billingslea
Doggy Revenge © 2012 Valerie D. Benko
We All Shine On © 2011 Dennis C. Bentley
The Runt © 2012 Ireta Black
Shiver Me Timbers © 2012 Carol Ann Brosowske
The Great Escape © 2012 Sallie Lyla Brown
The Dutch Progeny © 2011 Kathleen M. Campbell
Speck © 2012 Barbara Carpenter
Dream Girl © 2010 Elynne Chaplik-Aleskow
Canine in a Car © 2012 Carol L. Clouse
Big Red © 2012 Mark Crider
Side by Side © 2012 Mark Crider
Finding Pau's Marble © 2012 Jerry W. Davis
Special Delivery © 2012 Jerry W. Davis
Choosing Her Chews © 2012 Theresa J. Elders
There's a Pit Bull in My House © 2010 Joanne Faries
We Danced © 2009 Patricia R. Frank
Life is Good © 2012 Eve Gaal
The Right Doorstep © 2012 Joanne Gardner
Thalia © 2011 Betty Guenette
Sent Packing © 2012 Renee A. Hughes
Buddy's Pride © 2012 Betty Keel
Trusting Tanner © 2007 Rebecca Kragnes
The Beagle That Came In from Out of the Rain © 2012 Gregory Lamping
The Dog Whisperer Shakes His Head © 2012 Gregory Lamping
I Love Lucy © 2012 Linda Ann Lohman
Sunny Day © 2005 Rolland Love
Jake © 2012 Gladys Martin
Love Bites © 2012 Kenneth McKowen
Stop, Thief! © 2010 Gina L. Mulligan

Photo Permissions

Publishing Syndicate

Publishing Syndicate LLC is an independent book publisher based in Northern California. The company has been in business for more than a decade, mainly providing writing, ghostwriting and editing services for major publishers. In 2011, Publishing Syndicate took the next step and expanded into a full-service publishing house.

The company is owned by married couple Dahlynn and Ken McKowen. Dahlynn is the CEO and publisher, and Ken serves as president and managing editor.

Publishing Syndicate's mission is to help writers and authors realize personal success in the publishing industry, and, at the same time, provide an entertaining reading experience for its customers. From hands-on book consultation and their very popular and free monthly *Wow Principles* publishing tips e-newsletter to forging book deals with both new and experienced authors and launching three new anthology series, Publishing Syndicate has created a powerful and enriching environment for those who want to share their writing with the world. (www.PublishingSyndicate.com)

NYMB Needs Your Stories!

We are looking for hip, fun, modern and very-much-today type stories, just like those in this book, for 30 new titles in the *NYMB* series. Published contributors are compensated.

Submission guidelines at www.PublishingSyndicate.com

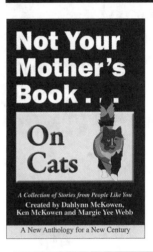
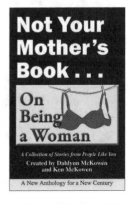
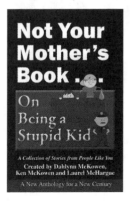

More *NYMB* Titles

Look for new
Not Your Mother's Books
coming soon!

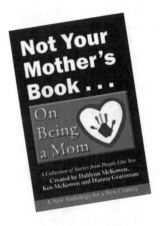

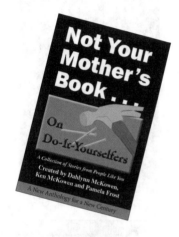

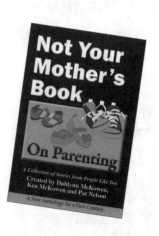

Parents, do your kids like to write?

OMG! My Reality! For Teens

Publishing Syndicate is now accepting stories for our new teen book series!

This new anthology will feature a collection of personal real-life stories written by and about teens. We are looking for humorous, heart-warming and inspiring stories **written by individuals 25 years and younger about their teen experiences.**

If your kid has a story to share about a personal experience that will touch the hearts, lives and souls of other teens, we would love to consider it for publication in *OMG! My Reality! For Teens*. Royalties will be paid to those whose stories make the book. And being a published author is a great accomplishment to add to college and job applications. For more information and to read submission guidelines, visit our website.

We are also accepting stories for *OMG! My Reality! For Kids* and for *OMG! My Reality! For Preteens.*

www.PublishingSyndicate.com